TONE SETTERS

IN THE ACADEMY

PUBLISHED BY AVOCET BOOKS
www.avocetbooks.com

ISBN:

eBook	978-1-963678-06-2
Paperback	978-1-963678-07-9

First Edition

BOOK PRODUCTION BY HAL CLIFFORD ASSOCIATES
www.hcabooks.com

TONE SETTERS

IN THE ACADEMY

*How to Build an Inspired Life
as a University Administrator*

ANDREW TRACY CEPERLEY

Praise for *Tone Setters in the Academy*

"*Tone Setters in the Academy* is an insightful playbook for current and aspiring university administrators, highlighting how inspirational leaders create positive campus cultures while curating their own energy, growth, and path to wisdom. Through practical examples and reflective frameworks, Andrew Ceperley offers valuable advice for transforming a career in higher education from a mere job into a fulfilling vocation."

—CHIP CONLEY, *New York Times* bestselling author and Founder of the Modern Elder Academy

"Is there a better time for a book like this? Confidence in our institutions of higher education is slipping, and considerable ire is directed at them from Congress, donors, parents and, of course, the students themselves. Along comes this charming gem packed with insightful stories, practical advice and, yes, hope culled from the author's own journey as a university administrator. *Tone Setters in the Academy* may have been written as a teaching memoir, and those in higher education will find much to learn from this playbook, but you don't have to be in academia to admire and enjoy it (as I did immensely)."

—KOPIN TAN, writer and former Dow Jones journalist

"In *Tone Setters in the Academy*, the wise and engaging Andrew Ceperley offers indispensable guidance for university administrators (and those who aspire to be), blending real-world examples with practical advice to inspire and elevate their careers. This book serves as a valuable and timely blueprint for creating positive campus cultures and transforming higher education roles into deeply fulfilling vocations."

—LINDSEY POLLAK, *New York Times* bestselling author of *Becoming the Boss: New Rules for the Next Generation of Leaders*

"If you work for a college or university, setting the right tone can feel like the job of a lifetime. Unless you discover the magic of doing the work and loving your contributions, large and small, your campus can feel confusing, isolating, and melodramatic. Andrew Ceperley provides us a path forward as staff members, one where we add our own authentic value while discovering who we are and how we are meant to serve. If you are questioning your place in higher education administration, this is a must read."

—STUART E. SCHWARTZ, Ed.D., professor and author

"Andy Ceperley has inked a profoundly inspiring and useful book about how to be successful, engaged, and fulfilled in one's career. I cannot wait to recommend it to a diverse array of individuals at every stage of their careers; even those outside of academia. The material is a beautiful blend of strategy and storytelling from the perspective of a man who has clearly 'walked the walk.'"

—JORDAN MANESS, M.Ed., Certified Life Coach, Career Advising
Specialist, creator and instructor for Coursera's *Thriving 101: Designing a Fulfilling Life & Career*, Author *Select An Ideal Life (SAIL): Your 59-Minute Guide to Enjoying the Journey of Life*

"Very few of us who become university administrators would have said that was what we wanted to be when we grew up. Finally, we have the book we have needed to navigate that impactful profession, whether just starting out or as a seasoned professional. Andrew Ceperley, a true visionary, uses examples from his own experience, combined with wisdom gained over years of working in a variety of universities, to lay out a series of astute and succinct mindsets. These both prompt self-assessment and promote an expansive perspective of work that is consequential and profound. This insightful book is for anyone who wants to elevate full possession of themselves and, in so doing, become a significant Tone Setter."

—CATHERINE NEINER, higher education consultant

"*Tone Setters in the Academy* is dedicated to educational administrators advancing their careers on college and university campuses. Author Andy Ceperley weaves in personal experiences coupled with examples from colleagues that sets the stage for understanding Tone Setters. Andy's personal stories inspire and build a bond between reader and author. We are reminded that flaws and failures are as much a part of us as our assets and successes. Andy does this with humor, encouragement and a finger on the pulse of our institutions."

—SUSAN TERRY, career strategist, consultant, and transition specialist for the University of Washington Retirement Association

"Sometimes we pursue our calling with clarity and intention. Other times, we stumble into it, drawn by forces we don't understand. *Tone Setters in the Academy* is a love letter to the former, to all those accidental university administrators who, through luck or circumstance, discover a career that fills them with a sense of pride and purpose. Elegantly weaving together personal stories with astute observations and actionable takeaways, author Andrew Ceperley unpacks his own journey so that others can find success in theirs. Through this book, readers will learn to embrace their roles and grow in their work, becoming the tone setters so vital to a thriving campus. Reading this book, I couldn't help but pine for my own days as a campus employee. More importantly, I found new appreciation and gratitude for the myriad Tone Setters who supported me during my own academic journey. What a great read!"

—CHAS HOPPE, founder, Cape & Cowl Media

"It's unusual to read two books in one; however, that's what it feels like to me. The first is a magical and rich memoir of a life in higher education; the other is an excellent guidebook for anyone who wants to be a more effective leader in any field. Ceperley delights us with stories from a broad swath of college campuses brought to life by his years of experience. He simultaneously takes us on a journey of discovery and awareness building, inviting us to explore and expand our impact in the world."

—Cynthia Darst, Author and Master Certified Coach (MCC)

"Never has someone so eloquently explained why die-hard college administrators love higher education as we do despite the long hours, the personal politics, and the historical slow pace of change. *Tone Setters in the Academy* is an unexpected and artfully written playbook for post-secondary staffers who are tired and stuck but dedicated and passionate about the work they do and the people they do it for. Andrew Ceperley's book belongs in every conference room where higher-education teams convene. Complete with mindset tips, reflections, and exercises, *Tone Setters in the Academy* is a book that gets things done for the people who get things done in higher education. Thought-provoking, reassuring, inspiring, practical, honest, and entertaining in a way that few books for higher-ed staffers have ever been."

—Kate Colbert, higher-education marketing consultant and ladership coach, and Author of *Commencement: The Beginning of a New Era in Higher Education*

"There is a question I have asked myself since I was a child—when does a person become wise? After reading Andrew Tracy Ceperley's *Tone Setters in the Academy* I have a much better understanding of how wisdom informs the work we do on our campuses. Through sharing stories of personal experiences as a university administrator and the many wise people he encountered along the way, Ceperley shines a light on the important contributions of academic administrators to the education of the students entrusted to us at our colleges and universities. From the allure of the college campuses he visited in high school, to his professional growth as a national leader in higher education, to the inspiring wisdom of his father, a college professor, Ceperley tells his stories with grace and gentle humor, showing us how we can all be tone setters in the academy."

—JANE MORRIS, executive director of the Center for Undergraduate Research and Fellowships, University of Pennsylvania

"*Tone Setters in the Academy* should be required reading for everyone in higher education and those aspiring to enter the field. Andrew Ceperley lays out a blueprint for how to get college campuses and college administrators flourishing again, emphasizing how higher education professionals can reconnect with the reasons they entered the field in the first place. This is an excellent read, filled with vibrant stories, compelling themes, and valuable lessons. Andy provides practical advice based on his extensive experience on many campuses, offering a refreshing perspective on how to invigorate the academic community. His insights are not only inspiring but also actionable, making this book a must-read for anyone dedicated to the advancement and enrichment of higher education."

—LEE KRAMER, Master Certified Life Coach and former university student life director

*For my parents, Gerry and
Gordon "Cep" Ceperley.*

*They gave me all I needed
to set my tone and run with it.*

CONTENTS

PREFACE

S TANDING IN THE cavernous ballroom at Orlando's World Center Marriott, I looked around the cool, dim, empty space. Over two thousand chairs were positioned symmetrically on a jewel-toned patterned carpet, facing a platformed stage far in the distance with its bigger-than-life Jumbotrons covering the walls on either side. I padded silently up the center aisle as a production crew of six men busily adjusted stage lights and ran music cues.

My ears picked up the sound of a growing roar in the back of the room behind banks of locked doors that opened up to the lobby, where a crowd of conference attendees was gathering for the opening plenary session. In five minutes, those doors would open and the ballroom would quickly fill with the energy of people from all over the world, each of them with their own unique relationship to the industry of higher education. But for now, in the silence before the commotion, I tried to breathe in the quiet hum of the air-conditioning system and cherish this moment, the only moment just like this one I would ever experience.

"Are you Andy?" a disembodied voice from the sound system asked, jerking me out of my haze. "I will be your VOG."

"I'm sorry, what?" I asked as I looked behind me, in front of me, and all around to get a visual of where the voice was coming from.

"VOG. It means Voice of God," the commanding voice added as a man in a baseball cap waved from an elevated production platform in the back of the ballroom. "I will be announcing you to the audience as you take the stage for your welcome speech. I see that your name is spelled C E P E R L E Y. Is that right?"

"You got it," I replied, pleasantly surprised as so few have ever managed to get that spelling correct on the first try.

"OK then," he said. "I'll practice it a few times. I don't want to butcher your name." He chuckled.

"Thanks, me neither," I replied, wondering why VOG hadn't asked for a phonetic spelling in the first place.

Another tech appeared from the front of the room to wire me for amplification, beginning the awkward and strangely intimate experience of unbuttoning my dress shirt, dropping a cold microphone wire down to my waist, and experimenting with different locations to clip the receiver. His hands guided the equipment to various choice spots, moving it from my butt to my hip and ultimately clipping the device with satisfaction on my belt buckle, ever so close to my groin.

"Could you at least buy me dinner first?" I joked clumsily.

The AV tech ignored me before deadpanning, "You will want to be sure to turn this little puppy off if you use the john. Otherwise a thousand of your best friends will hear you pee and flush."

I thought of how incredibly mortifying that would be.

The VOG boomed from the back, "Presenting your 2013 association president ... Andrew *Keperley*!"

"How was that?" VOG asked.

"It's a soft *C*, not a *K*," I shouted.

"OK. Sorry. Let's try it again," VOG replied.

"Presenting your 2013 association president ... Andrew *Seperelli!*" the disembodied voice boomed, landing the soft *C* with perfection but making my name sound Italian. It's not.

"Nope," I responded, my mic now operational and my voice filling the ballroom as if I were Voice of God's competing Voice of Satan.

"Is it *Craperley*?" VOG replied.

"Seriously?" I murmured, incredulous, my jet lag morphing into annoyance as I relived childhood taunting. Then, in a fit of helpfulness, I offered this for all two thousand empty chairs to hear: "It sounds a bit like the words *separately* or *celery*."

"Oh, cool, that helps!" VOG responded. "I'll make a note of that."

I wasn't convinced.

Eventually, our sound checks were completed, the house lights were brought up, and blazing spotlights swept the stage as if at a Hollywood premier, pinpointing the massive, bigger-than-life conference logo that read GREAT WORK! Three non-gendered, cartoonish stick figures in orange, blue, and green stood atop the text, their arms stretched to the sky like those balloon figures at car dealerships. I supposed they were depicting an animated version of the jubilation one feels when immersed in what can only be described as great work.

My quiet moment ended. I was ushered backstage by the AV tech as the doors opened and attendees moved into the ballroom to take their seats for the annual meeting of NACE, the National Association of Colleges and Employers.

There in the wings, in the dark, I could hear the rising hum of the growing audience as the Kelly Clarkson hit of the day, "Catch My Breath," blasted from the sound system.

Then the music stopped, and I could hear the settling murmur of the audience. From where I stood backstage left, I could see a spotlight pinpointing a pool of light on center stage. Despite years of public speaking under my belt, my heart pounded as if this were the first time.

My tech nudged me. "We are ready for you," he whispered calmly in my ear, turning my microphone receiver to *on* as he nudged me toward the light.

The commanding Voice of God filled the ballroom. "Ladies and Gentlemen, please take your seats and welcome to the stage your 2013 NACE president ... Andrew **Ceperley**!"

He got it right!

I stepped out from the shadows and onto my mark in the spotlight, my heart pounding as I waved to the applauding audience. I looked down at a large teleprompter as my prepared script started its scroll, and I began opening a conference I never imagined I would convene in an industry in which I never imagined I would work.

How in the world did I get here?

INTRODUCTION

I'VE LOVED THE ENERGY of a college campus since I first set foot on one during a high school college tour. I can think of no other place that so elegantly assembles people from a diversity of backgrounds and generations for two inspired goals: to teach and to learn. It's hard to argue with either one. For me, the places where these interlinked activities happen are like miniature, verdant landscapes specifically designed to enable the interplay of wide-eyed learners with the scholarship, rigor, and networks of those paid to fill their minds and facilitate their personal and professional success. Everyone flourishes.

Of course, when I was in college, it did not occur to me that my alma mater, so timely about invoicing me for tuition payments, might one day actually pay me a living wage to stay put after I graduated, jump-starting a surprising career that would in the following decades fuel my fascination with college and university administration. What seemed like a temporary gig after graduate school spiraled into professional opportunity and personal growth.

Let's be honest—any of us who found ourselves employed by colleges and universities could have pursued professions in any number of industries, right? We could have followed the leads of our classmates from senior year in college, caving to peer pressure by pursuing more practical careers in manufacturing, high tech, finance, or consulting. Instead, and for reasons that are highly personal to each of us, we chose higher education and made the academy a primary benefactor of our life's work.

College and university administrative careers can be intoxicating professional choices, and for some very good reasons.

The rhythm of higher education is familiar
Most of us spend the bulk of the first twenty-two years of our lives as students, moving lockstep through educational systems that afford us regular performance feedback, annual promotions, and a near-guaranteed sense of progression.

Our campus colleagues are extraordinary
We work alongside an incredibly diverse mix of creative, eccentric, and brilliant professionals. Our faculty and researchers are wedded to their disciplines and the new knowledge they bring forth. Our admissions teams invent new approaches to recruitment, our student life staff members devise novel strategies to strengthen student integrity, and our coaches find ways to integrate the competitive spirit of athletes with the rigorous requirements of the classroom.

Campus perks are abundant
Those of us who work on college campuses may be able to earn tuition credits for ourselves or our families. We may have free or low-cost access to daycare, a gym membership, a transportation supplement, and even legal and retirement advice.

Youth springs eternal
Higher education administration keeps us young at heart, hip to the latest trends popularized by a younger generation and inspired by the transformative once-in-a-lifetime experience that our students, like us, will never forget.

The campus rounds out a full life
Within a short walk from our office, we can take in a lecture by an internationally recognized scholar, relax with a great book in a world-class library, check out a new exhibit at our art museum, run on the track at the fieldhouse, buy school swag at the bookstore, and take in a musical in our campus theater.

Higher education is noble

We are doing good work in an organization where the bottom line is not an increase in sales or a hopeful IPO but instead the growth and social transformation of others. An August 2023 report from Gallup and the Lumina Foundation found that higher education improves outcomes beyond employability and earnings, demonstrating a positive impact on personal health, civic engagement, and even relationships.

Tell an acquaintance that you work at your local university, and the response you get nine times out of ten will be, "Wow, that's cool! What do you teach?" Once you overcome your annoyance and master your tightened retort that you don't teach but are a director of a particular unit on campus, you can explain the truth: the vast majority of employees on campus are not teaching faculty. They are administrators, like you and me, vital contributors who enhance the student experience, manage the infrastructure, and keep our academies humming.

Perhaps you are considering a career in higher education administration and are trying to discern if it is a good move for you. Or maybe you are a higher-ed practitioner in the middle of your career and are beginning to question your professional path or contemplating next steps. Or it could be that you are nearing retirement and wishing to exit with a meaningful legacy.

Reflect with me for a moment. What do you suppose makes an administrative career at a college or university a good fit for you?

Is it:

- A tangible feeling of your positive impact on college students?
- A convenient, flexible, and forgiving career as you raise your family?
- A side hustle while you work on your doctoral dissertation?
- A way to relive your own halcyon college days?
- A gentle escape from the corporate rat race?
- An opportunity to step off the tenure track and pursue work that provides greater stability?

Perhaps like you, I was lured to a career in college administration for some of these same reasons. And now, after decades in the business, I serve as a coach to college and university academic and staff practitioners and their teams. From newer administrators to senior leaders with broad responsibilities and complex portfolios, I assist people looking to inspire their work with innovation, energy, and authenticity. I have worked on, consulted with, and toured nearly a hundred campuses in the United States, Canada, Australia, New Zealand, Germany, Poland, South Africa, and the Philippines. I've worked for professors, vice chancellors, academic deans, fundraisers, admissions directors, and chief student affairs officers. I've shared meals with trustees and donors, glad-handed alumni, and traveled with presidents. I've chatted with and consoled parents, one couple whose child was tragically killed in one of the 9/11 plane crashes. Through all of it, I've grown to appreciate the intricacies of campuses with vastly different cultures and missions—from small private colleges to faith-based schools, public flagships, highly selective elites, and universities abroad.

My higher education career offered me highs beyond my wildest expectations. And it served up more than a few notable disappointments. I am proud of the cupboard in my coaching studio filled with my award certificates, plaques, trophies, and an engraved clock. I have been honored to serve on boards and to preside over a national association. I have been the "sage on stage" for many professional education programs. Some people have called me a star because of my professional commitment and communication style, while others sought my removal because of my identity. I've dutifully delivered countless performance appraisals to those who reported to me, and I have been on the receiving end of more than my share of 360-degree reviews from my boss. I have been rewarded with substantial pay increases and stipends, and I have shouldered dreaded pay cuts. I've been promised promotions in writing, and I have had them taken away before the ink of the offer signature was dry. I've onboarded and mentored new staff right out of graduate school, and I have eulogized those who came before me and left us too soon. I guess you might say that I have soared on the wings of success and that I have sampled the sour taste of humble pie—yearning for my campus job to be eternal during the good times and cursing my professional choices when my zest for the work evaporated.

Yet for all the peaks and valleys, there was this hunger deep inside me, nudging me beyond the situation of the day toward aspirational stretch roles, jobs that would offer me broader scope and higher stakes. I thrive on constant movement. Getting from A to B has always mattered to me. The journey and the destination motivate me equally. As a kid, I enjoyed taking long walks with my mother in the arboretum near our suburban Philadelphia home. Mom's walking stick in hand, we would stroll briskly in a massive loop, taking in the seasonal foliage. My father was a motion junkie as well. When he moved our entire family to Israel for a year, he would make an adventure out of routine drudgery. I can still remember trying to keep up with him as my three older brothers and I trudged behind our dad on Jerusalem's Mount of Olives, heavy satchels of dirty clothes balancing precariously on our heads. Our destination was the nearest laundromat on the other side of the mountain.

Throughout this book, I'll use stories from my personal experience to shine light into the nooks and crannies of our campus roles. So many that I have worked alongside and coached are college administrators by happenstance, their names appearing in boxes on a university org chart, set smack in the middle of the page with layers of boxes above and layers below, pursuing their purpose in this vast world of higher education, a storied industry employing nearly five million workers and responsible for the education of ten million undergraduate students in the United States alone.

Wherever my work takes me, I find myself in the presence of college and university administrators with whom I share an immediate bond. I respect them immediately for what they are trying to accomplish. Like me, they are drawn to their work and eager to make their unique imprint on it. They want to strengthen their influence muscles. They strive to ensure that what they do truly matters and is in alignment with their values. In essence, they wish to be more than mere college administrators. They desire to live authentically as tone setters in the academy.

So, who are these tone setters I reference? Fortunately, on any college campus, we are surrounded by a vast array of tone setters. They are quite literally all around us. Tone setters in our academies can be found among our administrative assistants, resident advisers, campus police officers, athletic coaches, technology specialists, and custodians. They can be our presidents, deans, provosts, and directors. Tone setters are defined less by their career choices or positional authority than by their wise characteristics.

Tone setters pursue their work with fulfillment and impact. They act as though where they are is where they are meant to be at this moment. Ask a tone setter how they feel about trading in their higher education career for another industry and they will likely respond, "Why would I do that? This is my professional home. This is where I belong."

Tone setters create ambience for those they are called to serve and lead. They raise the dimmer switch. They shape experiences, add texture, and paint color onto their work. They level up the workplace with their affirming presence, eternal curiosity, and quiet generosity. They may not have the highest standardized test scores of those sitting around the conference table at the weekly staff meeting, but our tone setters are often the wisest. Their personalities range from over-the-top characters to quiet, nuanced accomplishers. They may be assigned roles as designated campus leaders. Or they may make their impact from below or within the hierarchy. They may be influencers on social media, or their Instagram feed may simply feature adorable cat videos.

This concept of tone is all around us, right? The new lounge furniture in your student center sets a tone: comfort. The colleague who annoyed you in a Zoom staff meeting last week sets a tone: abrasive. The cluttered office of your faculty chair sets a tone: absent-minded. The roaming parking attendant who ticketed your car last week sets a tone: ugh!

The chime of your campus carillon at noon sets a tone: sentimental. Your president's executive assistant who answers the phone with a cheery "Good morning, how may I help you?" sets a tone: reliable.

Tone is also engrained in our personal style. It's the tone of our voice: its quality, pitch, and volume. It is the pace of our steps and the brightness in our eyes. "I don't like your tone," my mother would scold when I was being a bratty kid. Or when we "open mouth, insert foot," as the expression goes, we are labeled "tone deaf." Our language offers endless synonyms describing our tone—clarifiers like reedy, brassy, effervescent, dark, harsh, and clear.

So how do you discover, activate, and set your authentic tone as a college administrator? How do you manifest your tone, make it last, and stretch its elasticity as you grow in your wisdom on campus? As tone setters, we are called to find our tonal through line—how we see ourselves and how others receive us. Tone is a way of being more than a way of doing. It is presence over production, an alchemy of the many ingredients I will introduce in this book.

Tone Setters in the Academy drops into our lives as tone setters—our values, our purpose, and many of the lessons learned from my own career and the careers of those who trust me to be their coach. Whether you are early in your career, midway through, or considering a life pivot, the stories, methodologies, and mindsets shared in this book will construct a strong foundation and an achievable path forward in your higher education career.

In my view, you cannot separate tone setters from their physical environments. So I'll take you to some special campuses—from the historic steps of the Rotunda at the University of Virginia to the iconic tower at the University of Texas, the Gothic library at the University of Washington, the seaside eucalyptus grove at the University of California, San Diego, the urban landscape of Australia's University of Melbourne, and the meandering Mexican campus of the Modern Elder Academy. And I will introduce you to the behaviors and strategies of tone setters I have met and observed in those places.

This book is for you if you answer yes to any or all of these questions. Are you:

- Feeling stuck in the middle of your school's hierarchy—managing down, up, and across?
- Losing patience with the lack of promotional opportunities?
- Exhausted from what is increasingly feeling like a grind?
- Increasingly cynical as you count the days until retirement?
- Struggling to navigate the political complexities of a new administrative role?
- Disillusioned by your engagement with students, colleagues, supervisors, and direct reports?
- Wondering how you might develop new habits to strengthen your resilience?

Don't worry if you responded yes to more than a few of those. As we will explore in *Tone Setters in the Academy,* college and university administration is not the easiest life choice you could have made. All those charming benefits I shared can quickly lose their luster in the midst of political and financial instability, lack of clear career pathways, and growing debate about higher education's return on investment for students and for society as a whole. Now more than ever, in order to experience success as administrators, we need a new kind of playbook of deep self-awareness and insight well beyond job-specific baseline skills, kind hearts, and cozy nostalgia from our college days. In fact, we can adopt specific mindsets and recommit to what makes our work so vitally important, so aspirational, and so endlessly interesting. As I will argue, each of us is fully capable of becoming a tone setter in the academy.

In the chapters ahead, we will fly above ourselves as higher education tone setters from four perspectives. We will explore how to cultivate our tone, manage our energy, soften our rough edges, and grow into the multitude of possibilities that emerge in our lives on campus.

Most chapters conclude with what I refer to as tone setter mindsets, actionable strategies for you to adopt to more fully express your unique tone and enjoy your campus life more. Each chapter ends with a powerful question for you to consider as you apply the mindsets. We will also uncover tone setters' private and public wisdom characteristics, ways of being we can manifest through years of practice, lived experience, and comfort in our own skins.

I have an important request to make as we get started. I ask you to become an alert observer, reflecting without judgment but with abundant curiosity on your tone and the tone of those on your campus and in your sphere who baffle you, trigger you, and most especially inspire you. I want you to get present with your campus experience like never before, taking a magnifying glass to it like an anthropologist who has just unearthed an object of sacred value.

This book is not a "do as I do" manifesto. It's more of a "do as I observe" book as I share my observations from a higher education career spanning more than three decades. I think of myself as an alert observer. I have paid attention to the behaviors of those who, in their own ways, managed to light up a campus for me, making the mundane splendid and the impossible achievable. As an International Coaching Federation certified coach with hundreds of hours of direct client experience, I have come to understand the pain points of my campus clients' experience, and I help them to implement tested coaching principles to fix what's not working for them in their careers. Hopefully, they have learned from me. Without question, I have learned from them, and I proudly share their journeys and my observations as together we become tone setters in the academy.

PART ONE

CULTIVATING YOUR TONE

LOOK OUT OF YOUR OFFICE WINDOW at the start of fall semester, and you will witness a timeless ritual: the annual coming to life of the campus. Outside on freshly mowed grassy quads, harried students rush off to their 8:00 a.m. classes, wishing those classes were on Zoom and cursing the registrar for jolting them awake from their cozy dorm slumber. Each year, while you and I get older, those students remain frozen in the magical adulting age of eighteen to twenty-two.

What do the registrar and countless other college and university administrators think of their jobs? Their campuses? Their colleagues? Their lives? How do they emanate a tone of fresh enthusiasm for each crop of new students?

To be a tone setter, you'll need to develop your authentic tone, that hard-to-measure presence that brings something positive to your work and brightens the experience of those you lead, partner with, and ultimately serve. But how do you pull this off? Start by appreciating the history you are writing. Tap into your boundless capacity for engagement on the job. And discover what it takes to live a life of purpose.

CHAPTER 1

HISTORY

Appreciate Your Role in the Story

If you want to understand today,
you have to search yesterday.
—Pearl S. Buck

W HEN DOES THE HISTORY of your college or university begin? How far back do your traditions stretch? Your campus has a backstory. But why should you care about what happened before you arrived? A tone setter adopts the mindset that whatever their campus role, they are written in to their university's script. They are part of the story. So are you and I. We are there for a reason, and our understanding of what came before we arrived will help us cultivate our tone. In order to do that, we need to understand when and where the higher education story began.

Thousands of years before you or I stepped onto our respective college campuses, something was brewing in Greece. An institution of higher learning was in the works, thanks to Plato, arguably our industry's first tone setter. In 387 BC, his *Akademia* was located outside the city walls of ancient Athens in a grove of olive trees. It charged no tuition or membership fees. It offered no clear distinction between teachers and students, and there was no formal curriculum of any kind. Although it was open to the public, only upper-class men availed themselves of its program, one created to advance human knowledge through philosophical inquiry.

In the Middle Ages, the Catholic Church carved out its own knowledge niche, constructing early monastic and cathedral schools to facilitate intellectual exchange. Europe had become the epicenter of education, and academies were established to address this societal priority. The University of Bologna was founded in 1088, the University of Oxford in 1096, and the University of Paris in 1150. These universities laid an early foundation for academic disciplines, formalized curricula, and established degrees.

The Renaissance period in the fourteenth to seventeenth centuries saw a rising interest in the humanities, sciences, and arts. The invention of the printing press facilitated the spread of knowledge and led to the establishment of more universities across Europe. Scholars still familiar to us today, like da Vinci and Galileo, made groundbreaking contributions to their respective fields, epitomizing a spirit of inquiry. Developing one's thirst for knowledge became an aspiration and a reality for a growing number of privileged Christians.

Centuries later and an ocean apart, in Colonial America, higher education advanced in fast-forward, mirroring a new nation's Puritan values, pioneer spirit, and scrappy responsiveness to rapid and chaotic societal shifts. In 1636, a school was built in Massachusetts, and without much fanfare. It was this country's first postsecondary academy, called Harvard College. Soon after, similar institutions were established, including Yale, William & Mary, and the College of New Jersey (now Princeton).

At first these schools consisted of little more than a small grouping of classroom buildings. The strategic addition of campus chapels kept young men laser-focused on broadening their minds and deepening their subservience to, and fear of, a sin-damning God. The landscapes on which these schools stood came to be called college campuses, and they were tucked in remote regions of Colonial America, at least by today's urban standards, so as to avoid the vices associated with large towns and cities.

As America grew, so did its fascination with higher education, especially during war times. Following the American Revolution, nearly fifty new college campuses were built by the 1820s, all still purporting Christian values, though to a lessening extent over time. During this period, new kinds of structures called dormitories were constructed as a means of monitoring students' extracurricular lives and facilitating their academic mastery through memorization and recitation.

In 1862, the Morrill Land-Grant Acts were passed in the midst of the Civil War to respond to a growing national desire for institutions of higher learning to more broadly serve "the people" by teaching national priorities of practical skill development, agricultural expertise, and industrial research. Soon, men could earn credentials in the professions, including medicine, law, education, and of course ministry.

Former American University provost Scott Bass, in his book *Administratively Adrift*, describes another bump that occurred following the Spanish-American War in 1898 and the rise of an era of imperialism and US expansionism under the Teddy Roosevelt administration. Invention and innovation were enhanced by government support, and America's vision for the research university emerged, complete with notable boards of trustees, respected presidents, talented faculty, and a rising number of doctoral candidates. In just twenty years, between 1890 and 1910, enrollments on American college and university campuses nearly doubled.

Fast-forward to 1944, two world wars and a Great Depression later, when the GI Bill was introduced to help qualified veterans and their family members secure funds to cover costs for college. The resulting campus boom was unparalleled. New land grant universities were built, enrollment again exploded, and women were enrolling in universities in greater numbers and across more disciplines. This was a far cry from earlier social expectations that women limit their studies to teaching and nursing.

In the post-World War II era, access to higher education expanded dramatically throughout the world. Governments recognized the importance of higher education in driving economic growth and social mobility, leading to increased funding for higher education. This period also saw the emergence of community colleges and vocational institutions, providing accessible pathways for individuals seeking practical skills and training.

A few decades later, and on the eve of the Vietnam War, President John F. Kennedy established the Consumer Bill of Rights "to be safe, to be informed, to choose, and to be heard." Americans were promoted from being mere citizens to becoming more vocal citizen customers. On our campuses, college students and their families grew to expect more campus features. New out-of-the-classroom programs and services emerged, including career placement, study abroad, student clubs and activities, campus recreation, and alumni affairs. As students and their families shifted their mindsets from learners who *earned* degrees to customers who *purchased* education, our campuses became platforms for lively discourse and sometimes violent protest—a free speech movement at UC Berkeley in 1964, administration building takeovers at Duke and Cornell in 1969, an anti-war demonstration at Kent State in 1970, and countless others in the years to follow.

Following the assassination of Kennedy, President Lyndon Johnson in a symbolic gesture returned to Texas State University, his alma mater, to sign into law the Higher Education Act of 1965, a sweeping policy that increased federal funding to universities, creating scholarships and offering low-interest loans to students. As Johnson argued to Congress, "Higher education is no longer a luxury but a necessity."

It was during this period that nonfaculty campus administrative roles expanded exponentially, marking the dawn of such massive nonfaculty staff growth that it became labeled with the pejorative term "administrative bloat." Tuitions rose, and financial aid became a necessity for millions of students who otherwise could not afford a college education. Extracurricular service offices continued to expand as school missions broadened—with significant nonfaculty growth in areas such as residence life, deans of students, instructional technology, advancement, disabilities services, ombuds, legal services, and women's centers (precursors of today's LGBTQ+ and cultural centers).

Any of us serving on a campus today is riding a wave that became a tsunami as baby boomers poured onto our grassy quads in the 1960s and 1970s—to get a job, to dodge the draft, to marry up, or to "fight the Man with flower power."

In the generations to follow—Generation X, millennial, Generation Z, and today's newest generation—our administrative roles continued to grow, and our departments expanded. Risk management and compliance offices attempted to prevent lawsuits. Fellowships and undergraduate research offices helped students apply their majors to the quest for new knowledge and postgraduate scholarship. Alumni engagement offices, advancement organizations, and athletic divisions inspired college loyalty, bolstered school spirit, and grew endowments. And new strategic roles were created, such as chief health officer, institutional planner, director of government relations, vice president for advancement, chief diversity officer, enrollment data specialist, director of teaching and learning, senior administrator for student success, director of residence life, chief information officer, chief information security officer, chief privacy officer, and countless others.

For these jobs, and nearly any other administrative campus roles we can think of, professional associations and societies were formed to connect our esoteric nonteaching campus roles with similar roles on other campuses. Over time, campus staff found themselves not merely working in administrative jobs but practicing in legitimatized professions for which academic degrees and specialized expertise mattered.

Collectively, administrators didn't come cheap. Bass describes the costly add-ons of student services alone, noting that these expenditures have more than doubled between 1987 and 2013 at private institutions, representing the largest sector increase of spending per student. At the same time, enrollments grew. Since 1980, the total number of undergraduates on our US campuses has swollen by 62 percent.

Our campus footprints grew as well, adding impressive student centers with inviting seating areas, quads, and grassy lawns with comfy Adirondack chairs; athletics complexes with indoor tracks;

coffee shops with vibey music for study and chat; and libraries with sprawling open spaces for students to gather in groups. These so-called sticky spaces in campus planning lingo transformed a mere collection of buildings into an artfully planned mini city.

Hollywood brought the college campus into popular culture with memorable films like *Animal House* (1978), *Good Will Hunting* (1997), *Legally Blonde* (2001), *The Social Network* (2010), and *Pitch Perfect* (2012). Pixar and Netflix have even added their take on higher ed with the animated *Monsters University* in 2013 and *The Chair* in 2021 when we were sheltered in our homes during the COVID-19 pandemic.

Traditions became an important means for universities to distinguish themselves from one another and to set a tone of spirit, belonging, and lightheartedness. Everyone at Clemson University knows that you come to campus on Fridays dressed in Clemson orange. And all self-respecting members of Purdue's community of Boilermakers know how significant it is to get their picture taken next to the school's big bass drum, reported to be the largest in the world. University of Oregon students learn the history of their huggable mascot, Puddles, with its striking resemblance to Disney's Donald Duck. Meanwhile, freshmen at California's University of Redlands commit to memory the school's congratulatory cheer, a nonsensical lyric that goes like this: "Orky Porky Dominorky. Redlands! Rah, Rah Redlands!"

Today, higher education institutions continue to evolve in response to technological advancements, societal needs, and global challenges. Online learning platforms and massive open online courses (MOOCs) enable individuals to access educational resources and courses from anywhere in the world, revolutionizing the traditional classroom-based model. The rise in artificial intelligence is also changing the way faculty teach and the way students learn. Interdisciplinary research, experiential learning, and institutional assessment add sophistication and practical strategy to students' campus experience.

WHERE WE ARE TODAY

And how are we feeling as college and university administrators at this moment in our history? All told, there are an estimated 4.7 million people employed by colleges and universities today. It remains a people-intensive enterprise, but it is showing signs of dysfunction.

Here are some sentiments I have heard from my coaching clients.

"Honestly, I am just working this campus job for the tuition benefits. Once I get my MBA, I am going corporate."
"I could be making so much more money elsewhere."
"I deserve a promotion, but there is no career path here."
"I am going nuts; this system moves so damn slowly."
"I've had five bosses in six years, and I am so tired of chasing another leader's fleeting pet projects."

Those sentiments are heartfelt. It's true—our campuses today can easily feel unstable and their histories overhyped. The politics and resource battles become constrictive and highly dramatized. According to a 2022 Hechinger Report, as an industry, higher education has the dubious distinction of having lost the confidence of the American public faster than any other institution measured by the Gallup polling organization. A July 2023 Gallup poll found that only 36 percent of Americans have "a great deal" or "quite a lot" of confidence in higher education, and this is down 20 percentage points from eight years earlier.

And that's not all. *New York Times* columnist David Brooks argues in a recent op-ed entitled "Death by a Thousand Paper Cuts" that campus administrative bloat may not be adding the value anticipated during those decades of growth. He writes, "The general job of administrators, who are invariably good and well-meaning people, is to supervise and control, and they gain power and job security by hiring more people to work for them to create more supervision and control."

Tone Setter Mindsets

Ouch! That's not what any of us signed up for, is it? Before you toss this book aside and retrain for a gig where you *think* you will be fully appreciated, take heart. Your professional opportunities in the academy will continue to grow—that is, if you are able to be agile in the midst of constant change with strong self-awareness and an eagerness to create and sustain value. Colleges and universities are stitched into the fabric of our cultures throughout the world. Our institutions may be showing their cracks, but staffed with the right tone-setting administrative talent, they will patch their flaws and flourish in new ways. And you may be just the tone setter to rise to the occasion.

Mindset #1

Learn your institution's timeline.

Whether your school is new or has a history dating back hundreds of years, your president's office, along with development and alumni affairs, have plenty of archival material highlighting the story of your campus and its many decision points leading to your arrival and current contributions. Knowing your institution's key milestones helps you contextualize the work you are doing today.

Mindset #2

Experience your campus through the eyes of a prospective student.

Have you reviewed your recent admission view book, seen the splashy new prospective student video, or attended an orientation kickoff? It doesn't matter if you are leading your school's finance office or preparing the student union for the new semester. You have a fresh audience arriving like clockwork each year for whom college is a once-in-a-lifetime experience. Take an admission tour and see if you can transport yourself back to that sensation when everything was brand new.

MINDSET #3

Investigate what's quirky and wonderful about your school's rituals.

What is higher education if not the keeper of tradition and ritual? TEDx speaker Tiu De Haan describes such rituals as "containers around a moment." Our campuses are filled with such containers. We wear our school colors with pride when it's time for welcome weeks, convocations, alumni weekends, or the big basketball game of the season. These traditions are a few of the experiences that bookmark our students' campus lives. Fully experiencing them yourself reminds you that you are part of your college's history.

MINDSET #4

Know the biographies of your institution's leaders.

I am often surprised when a coaching client doesn't know the name of their provost or the academic discipline of their president. "Oh, they play no role in my day-to-day," one client recently said to me. That may *appear* to be true, but in actuality our most visible and highly paid officials are the ultimate tone setters on our campus. We benefit from knowing who they are, attending their town halls, and understanding the goals of their strategic plans. The same holds true for your leadership board, trustees, and regents.

MINDSET #5

Read the news about higher education.

There are numerous daily publications and news feeds that feature up-to-the-minute highlights about people, events, and trends that are shaping higher education, from traditional media, like the *Chronicle of Higher Education* and *Inside Higher Education,* to more customized news channels for particular academic disciplines and campus functions. The more you understand our overall higher education context, the more your campus experience—and your satisfaction—will improve.

POWERFUL QUESTION

What would you like to create that is so valuable it will one day be featured in the narrative of your university?

CHAPTER 2

ENGAGEMENT
Discover Your Motivation

The world is full of magic things,
patiently waiting for our senses to grow sharper.
—W. B. Yeats

D O YOU REMEMBER the first time when you wondered, *Could I fit in in a place like this?* Each of us deserves the opportunity to feel part of our campus community, but the level to which we engage is up to us. It's beyond our position description, our annual performance appraisal, or what others expect of us day-to-day. Our engagement is ours to discover.

The University of Virginia

From my perch overlooking Charlottesville, my eyes were drawn to the sprawling University of Virginia campus below—with its lush central lawn, grand colonnades, and iconic white-domed rotunda with the massive white staircase leading to its portico. It did not occur to me that I was taking in the same view Thomas Jefferson did over two hundred years before, when from the north terrace of his mountaintop home at Monticello, where I stood, he would peep through his telescope to oversee the finishing touches of what he believed to be his greatest accomplishment, the founding of a university in 1819. Jefferson called his masterpiece an Academical Village, created to advance human knowledge, educate leaders, and cultivate an informed citizenry.

But as I took in the view that muggy August day, my thoughts weren't nearly as inspired as Jefferson's. Rather, I was feeling a bit anxious. I had just submitted my master's thesis in rhetoric and communication studies, taking the required ruler to my margins and ensuring perfect pagination to avoid the horror of a rejected manuscript. I was also turning in my apron as a visitor services specialist at Monticello, a part-time job that provided me with a little spending money while I was in graduate school. The next day, as a freshly minted MA from what to this day is referred to as Mr. Jefferson's University, I would begin my new job as resources manager and publicity coordinator in the Office of Career Planning and Placement (OCPP), my first exposure to higher education's endless fascination with abbreviations and acronyms. Actually, my university title for payroll purposes was the ego-deflating clerical *library assistant II*, loftier than a *library assistant I* but without the supervisory or budget expectations of the coveted *library assistant III*.

Less than three years before, I was living the Washington, DC, early career dream, on track to be a buyer for the Hecht Company, one of the nation's biggest department store chains at the time. But I remember clearly standing in the parking lot in front of Hecht's Landover Mall store one day, the roar of the DC Beltway just beyond as it raced through suburban Maryland, thinking that I was not in the right place. It was one of those intuitive hits in life, one that urged me to make a significant professional shift. So I resigned from Hecht's, determined to leverage the GREs I had taken and pursue a master of arts, a degree that though intellectually fascinating offered no clear professional outcome other than adding debt onto my yet-to-be-paid undergraduate loan from my bachelor's degree several years before.

Maybe you can relate. All of us who have built our professional reputations working on college campuses have origin stories about our early campus gigs. It is safe to say that few of us considered this work to be a professional aspiration during our undergraduate years. Still, many of us wax nostalgic about our own college experiences. Maybe for you it was a roommate in the dorm and a lifelong friendship that followed or an unforgettable professor in a literature class. Or perhaps it was a transformative study abroad semester or that part-time work-study job on campus that turned out to be incredibly fun. Maybe it was that time you partied too hard and found yourself on the wrong side of the student conduct code or the epic fraternity party where that compromising photo of you was taken. Or it could be the warm glow of your first big romantic love or your rebound from the heartbreak that all your friends knew would one day follow, if only you had listened. Rose-colored reflections of our college years somehow stick with us throughout our lives.

I, too, enjoy some warm memories of my undergraduate years at UVA's rival to the south, Virginia Tech, where I studied business but found my joy in the theater department. Yet here I was in the whiplash of my twenties, in my first full-time benefited campus job that paid $6,000 less per year than I was earning *before* I went back to graduate school. For a guy who took a job in a career office, of all places, it's ironic my own career made no sense, at least not yet.

"Andy, don't you think it's time to get a *real* job again, maybe back in DC where there are tons of opportunities?" a friend asked me. In truth, I did have my reasons for taking that first job at OCPP. Like so many that have made the transition from egg-headed grad student to modestly paid campus staffer, I made the choice less for professional aspiration or master plan than for what I believed to be a sensible response to the need for gainful employment. I was joining the ranks of overeducated Charlottesville townies, their egos puffed up from their elite credentials and their souls crushed by the uncertainty of how best to leverage them.

The words from my Hecht's supervisor upon my departure from retail years before rang in my head: "Andy, you need to find something you are really, really good at, then do it better than anyone else."

At age twenty-six, I had yet to discover what that was.

Maybe you can recall how you justified your first campus role. I tried to convince myself with affirming self-talk. After all, my esoteric degree in Aristotelian rhetoric in its purist form was about the art of persuasion. Maybe I could persuade myself. Perhaps a few years in an administrative campus gig could test my appetite for eventual PhD work, I thought.

Or maybe through a campus job I could earn my parents' pride. That made some sense. My mother, Gerry, was orphaned at a young age, grew up in a Long Island Christian foster care system, and at twenty married a promising twenty-six-year-old minister from Upstate New York. Pastor Gordon Ceperley would eventually become Professor Ceperley, making my three older brothers and me the ultimate APKs—academic preacher's kids. A college education was a nonnegotiable for us. In fact, our parents sold our family home to help finance our educations, along with plenty of scholarships and loans. Two of my brothers who are identical twins completed their undergraduate degrees side by side at Pennsylvania's Geneva College before serving in the Army. They went on and completed medical technology degrees at Thomas Jefferson University. My oldest brother joined a fraternity at Dickinson College, studied abroad for a year in Italy, and ultimately completed a master's degree at Georgetown University and a JD from Loyola Law School. All the while, our mother, who never earned a college degree, quenched her intellectual thirst by being our most voracious reader, a book always by her side.

Yet even with an upbringing of school, service, and faith, I was feeling the palpable anxiety of starting over with no clear direction of how best to define, pursue, and secure my own version of success. I didn't really know what success was for me.

UVA's Garrett Hall is where my higher education career begins—burrowed in my windowless, subterranean office in this historic building, circa 1908, steps from where both Edgar Allan Poe and Katie Couric once resided as students in still-treasured historic lawn rooms on the university's Central Grounds. I felt a paradox of emotions. On the one hand, I felt shame over this foray into what appeared to be underemployment. *Just what the world needs*, I thought cynically, *another MA with nowhere to go, the ultimate failure-to-launch story.* On the other hand, I felt a fierce determination to make the best of it. I told myself there was plenty to learn.

It turns out there was.

To my surprise, I grew to enjoy what I was doing day-to-day. I liked how I felt doing the work. I appreciated the bustling pace of the academic calendar and the creative energy of my colleagues. They were producing events, counseling students, teaching classes, and developing career content for job-seeking graduates. I found university life complex, confusing, and endlessly fascinating.

When it came right down to it, campus life was comfortable for me, and it was far gentler than my two-year foray into department store retail. I was reminded that on a college campus, semesters pass with the seasons. And academic years are punctuated with natural beginnings, middles, and ends—complete with the marching band playing "Pomp and Circumstance" as we wave graduates into their adult lives. The ebb and flow of students energizes the campus with the vitality of learners who are experiencing the most transformative rite of passage in the first quarter century of their lives. It then nudges them into their untested futures, emptying the campus in preparation for the next crop.

I liked developing an expertise that students valued. In my previous retail life, there was value too for sure. But at Hecht's, I was pushing products that people were convinced to desire. I was driving revenue. At the university, I was adding something intangible yet powerful to a student's experience. I replaced daily revenue reports with student development programs and bustling shopping malls with a sprawling college campus. It felt wholesome. I felt wholesome.

POSITIONS AS BEGINNINGS

So I learned my job, and over time I performed it well, thanks to a now-engrained work ethic modeled by my father and the inspiration of Thomas Jefferson's quotation I hung on my wall: "I'm a great believer in luck, and I find the harder I work the more I have of it."

My filed-away *library assistant II* position description was merely a beginning for me. Without expectation of financial reward, I pursued any and all professional development opportunities that my director tossed my way. Dr. Larry Simpson was a surprising administrator to me and my first tone setter of merit. Before I met Larry, I had the image in my head of a befuddled professor in a tweed sports coat. Larry was anything but that! He was trim and stylish, moving swiftly through the office in his crisp custom suits, greeting hello to his staff of seventeen with his charming Alabama accent and the woody fragrance of high-end cologne trailing behind him. Somehow, Larry saw in me a restless, self-absorbed up-and-comer who shared his hunger for innovation. He was ahead of his time in campus administration, dismissing the limitations of our state-funded budget and building a healthy supplemental income stream from parents, alumni, and employers who were more than willing to sponsor student career planning brochures, job search magazines, and a collection of videotapes demonstrating the art and the science of successful job interviewing.

Under Larry's mentorship, I consumed the *Chronicle of Higher Education* cover to cover when it landed in my office mailbox each week. I wrote articles for the student newspaper and a slew of student throwaway rags that cluttered campus newsstands. I overcame my tech phobia and learned early Macintosh design applications, mastering once-trendy clip art and developing hundreds of promotional pieces that to this day remain stored behind sheet protectors in massive binders in my coaching studio.

Larry's associate director, Karen Knierim, also set an affirming tone for me, complementing his administrative savvy with the care of a teacher and counselor. Karen walked me through our expansive career library, pulling off the shelves a stack of must reads, like *What Color is Your Parachute?*, *Please Understand Me*, and *The Complete Job Search Handbook*. Karen taught me how to review student résumés and operate the once state-of-the-art VHS camcorder to tape students' practice job interviews. I voiced ads for our programs on the student-run radio station, WUVA, and I earned extra cash by teaching elective classes in public speaking and career development at UVA and at the nearby community college. I operated well beyond my pay grade by learning the ropes of daily student counseling walk-ins, student after student in fifteen-minute increments, polishing my active listen skills as I tried to offer the same helpful experience to my twelfth student at the end of the afternoon as my first.

Within a few years, Larry and I were "cutting a deal," a term he embraced as he loved to negotiate with his staff on anything related to budget or professional development. He gave me permission to attend my first national higher education conference in California. He paid for the registration and hotel. I paid for travel. Larry saw this as a win-win. Even at my paltry salary, so did I.

I was terribly overdressed as I stepped into the lobby of the San Francisco Hilton to join college administrators from throughout the country for three days of breakout sessions, keynote speakers, meals (three full sit-down meals each day—those days are long gone), and a memorable night out at the city's famed Exploratorium for my first conference cocktail reception. It was a heady business, that first conference. Little did I know that twenty years later I would serve as president of this body of practitioners.

With Larry's encouragement, I conducted campus visits in the years to follow under the auspices of benchmarking research for articles I was writing. Off I went to meet administrators at spectacular east coast schools, so very different in tone from UVA. I met with staff members at the College of William and Mary surrounded by the historic charm of Colonial Williamsburg; Harvard University with its historic yard and eclectic Cambridge neighborhood; and NYU, where the campus and Lower Manhattan comingle in a cityscape of purple school banners.

Each campus was so distinct, and each professional who gifted me their time was so kind and so genuine. Like Larry and Karen, each administrator I met demonstrated a hard-to-measure enthusiasm for their work. *What's up with these people?* I wondered. It is not that they were workaholics, but I found their commitment to their roles intoxicating. Their tone was welcoming, strategic, and proud. Some of them had been in the higher education business for years, while some were not much older than me. They described their work as much more than a job. It was almost as if they were describing some kind of deep engagement, a calling bigger than themselves.

If this reads to you as the ultimate old-school dues-paying story, you are correct. Higher education has historically trained and advanced staff who are willing to roll up their sleeves and do whatever it takes to enhance students' out-of-the-classroom experience. Just ask a vice president of student affairs, now a vital member of her president's cabinet, who not all that long ago was mediating roommate conflicts as a resident adviser. Or check in with the head of your alumni association who remembers the old days when he would unstack chairs and type nametags for events. Few duties are too small, and doing things for the good of the community with a humble and genuine spirit often yielded opportunity. It still does. For the tone setters who inspire this book, their job descriptions with all the embedded mandated HR jargon signify a launch into wide-open contribution and opportunity, never a mere list of duties and responsibilities. Their positions are beginnings, not endings.

THE PROMISE OF A COLLEGE CAMPUS

Mr. Jefferson's Academical Village in Charlottesville, and all those other campuses that inspired me as a new administrator, stand among three thousand college campuses in the United States, with thousands more around the world. I learned that these storied places are more than grades and lecture halls. Their impact is broader than the cliched sage on stage, dropping intelligence on eager GPA-driven students. In fact, these academies are places where students, staff, and faculty intertwine and grow—in the classroom, research lab, residence hall, and countless other spaces that make the college campus so special.

Maybe that's what eventually hooked me. It was the promise of higher education—aspirational, noble, self-important, and so entirely engaging. The future is wide open, out there somewhere beyond the safe bubble created for our students. Higher education is both gatekeeper and gateway, from its selectivity through admission to the vast world it serves up upon graduation. The pursuit of a college degree comes with a beginning, a middle, and yet another beginning—a magnificent launch into the unknown.

And the campuses that create a place for this promise somehow manage to integrate all we feel as humans—our fears, hopes, failures, anticipation, surprise, and even for many a sweet taste of success. As I met and worked alongside the early tone setters in my career, I realized that I had unwittingly stepped into a line of work that produced a magical alchemy to which no other career choice could compare.

By happenstance I discovered my life's work.

TONE SETTER MINDSETS

Whatever current or envisioned campus role drew you to this book, getting to a place where you feel fully engaged takes intentionality and steady focus. You've got to pay attention. Otherwise it is too easy to get lost in the day-to-day administrivia—like tackling budgets, navigating politics, and advising high-maintenance students, families, or staff. Yet it is within your reach to fully experience the richness of your unique campus and show up each day as the tone setter you are meant to be.

MINDSET #6

Know your university's vision, mission, and values.
Your senior administration has undoubtedly spent countless hours and significant money to develop bold identity statements for your campus community. They have formed committees and possibly even hired consultants to create powerful messages about your university's "why."

The same may be true for your division and even your office. Make these identity statements more than jargon on the school's website. Know them and consider how they connect with your own day-to-day contributions on campus.

MINDSET #7

Regularly read your campus news feed.

Pay attention to your school's narrative as articulated through its news feed and its student newspaper. Campus media and communications offices have become increasingly sophisticated in recent years. So have student journalists. E-newsletters, campus updates, alumni magazines, and social media communities make it easy to align your contribution with campus priorities. This helps you appreciate the complexity and the energy of your university.

MINDSET #8

Become a patron of your community events.

Broaden your engagement by taking in those spirited activities that draw a crowd and infuse your campus with creativity and innovative thinking. Early in my career, I was on a call with an acquaintance from another university. I know I was doing a bit too much whining about some work-related slight or disappointment when he stopped me and asked, "Andy, do you ever get out of your office and feed your brain in other ways?" My response was probably along the lines of "Please, I am far too busy for that!" Eventually, his words sunk in, and I started selectively attending free events easily accessible on the university's staff calendar. It opened me up to new layers of the institution.

MINDSET #9

Up your game with campus training and association involvement.

Career professionals in most industries don't have the same access to free and low-cost enrichment that you do. You will find camaraderie and inspiration by lifting your eyes up from your own campus realities to connect with others with whom you share a common interest. Local organizations as well as regional, state, and national associations expose you to the broader landscape of higher education. You learn how others get things done, and you discover shared professional pain points. Over time, you can move beyond attending meetings and conferences and serve on committees and task forces, deliver workshops, and even pursue volunteer leadership. You'll be surprised how much your professional engagement grows.

MINDSET #10

Get to know your most valuable unsung heroes.

It takes so many individuals to make our campuses hum. From frontline reception desk workers to landscapers and their ubiquitous leaf blowers, physical plant workers who fix our heat, custodial teams that empty our trash, and the folks in the gatehouse handing out parking passes. These contributors account for essential and admittedly underpaid roles that keep our communities safe, clean, and organized. And we wouldn't get on well without them. Pay attention to these workers, greet them with a wave and a smile, know them and their families by name, and treat them with the same respect they treat their senior leadership peers.

MINDSET #11

Broaden your impact beyond your assigned silo.

On all college campuses, large and small, there is a constant push-pull around what is centralized and what is decentralized. And it becomes far too cozy for us to find our safe bubble and live in it, whether the bubble is a particular school or college, a research center, an off-campus incubator, or any other budget area where many of our needs are met in our campus subsystem. "Oh, I'm sorry, I work in the law school. I don't get to campus much," I heard one client share. Or, "Those folks in University Advancement are totally in their own world. I see no value in interacting with them." Find ways to keep it fresh and your relationships growing by serving on campus-wide committees, attending lectures in surprising academic areas, marching with staff colleagues in the Martin Luther King parade, and showing up for major events that bring together a cross section of the campus community.

POWERFUL QUESTION

What are three things you can do to improve your engagement with your campus community?

CHAPTER 3

PURPOSE
FOLLOW YOUR COMPASS

*The two most important days in your life are the day you
are born, and the day you find out why.*

—MARK TWAIN

C OMING TO TERMS with the why of what we do as higher education professionals should be a no-brainer. We work for
employers who build their reputations on cultivating intellectual curiosity, experimentation, and personal growth. It's what they do.
Yet if we are not considering our tone, our campus careers may feel like
mere jobs for pay. Of course, they are that—we need to make a living
after all. But they can be much more. Our campuses provide a perfect
sandbox for us to play with our purpose and lock it in.

THE UNIVERSITY OF CALIFORNIA, SAN DIEGO

The sprawling campus sits in a forest of eucalyptus trees on a cliff above
the Pacific Ocean in the upscale beachy resort city of La Jolla. It spans
more than a thousand acres that once comprised Camp Matthews
Marine Corps Base. A few of the original mess halls and barracks still
remain, though they are dwarfed by hundreds of newer structures,
invoking the various architectural fetishes come to life by decades of
constant construction to keep pace with expanding enrollment.

To the east of UC San Diego, the I-5 Freeway speeds by on its way
to downtown San Diego and Tijuana, Mexico, just beyond. Boosterish
billboards line the meandering eight-lane ribbon. FIND YOUR INNER
DUDE IN AMERICA'S FINEST CITY, one promises. To the west are cliffs

dropping off to Black's Beach below, with its white fluffy sand and nude sunbathers. Surf-hungry students lucky enough to score their housing preferences prop their longboards outside their dorms to catch some waves between classes. It's totally sick!

I was thrilled to land a visible administrative role here with a large staff, ample resource discretion, and significant programmatic responsibility. As Dr. Joseph Watson, the towering and initially intimidating vice chancellor who recruited me, explained over our interview dinner, "Andy, UCSD is a fit for you if you want to make an impact at a place still trying to figure out what it wants to be when it grows up." Dr. Watson, or Joe as he asked people to call him, was describing a young campus within the ten-campus University of California system, one that was giving its older and more established UCLA and Berkeley siblings a run for their money. UCSD was on the rise, generating buzz for its unique residential college system and building steam as a player of worth in the blossoming Southern California biotech industry. And no one, not even the most senior administrator, could find the courage to refer to Dr. Watson as Joe. Out of immense deference, respect, and genuine affection, he was always Dr. Watson to us.

On a beautiful late afternoon as the misty marine layer rolled in over campus, I stood in the Career Center's austere two-story atrium lobby and looked out on our bustling entrance plaza with its umbrella tables and aspirational boulevard banners celebrating various professional successes of UCSD Tritons. My staff was busy assembling chairs in our hundred-seat presentation room for an evening information session conducted by recruiters from the CIA. UCSD had been a top recruiting campus for the agency for years.

But something seemed off to me. It was the kind of intuitive hit that felt like a tickle crawling up my neck. My eyes fixated on a group of students gathering on the plaza outside. Their coming together looked far more orchestrated than dorm besties running into each other on the way to the campus pub. The group started with three or four, then quickly doubled, then tripled in size. And then it became even more real. I noticed that a dozen of them were carrying what looked like human bodies slung over their shoulders wrapped in orange sacks. They started placing the life-size orange body bags around the double-door entrance to the center while the CIA recruiters watched with interest from inside.

I stepped outside. My anxiety was interrupted by a voice.

"Where is your moral compass?" a brazen protester in a wrinkled ill-fitting flannel shirt croaked as he approached me. He then proceeded to regale me with the atrocities committed by the United States intelligence community. "How can you open up our campus to human *annihilation*?" he asked, presenting his scruffy, unshaved face and unpleasant breath well within my personal bubble.

Moral compass? I wondered as I stepped back. You would think that as the grown-up in this situation I would have had a wise retort. This could have been a teaching moment. Much to my disappointment, I had nothing pithy to say other than to do my administrative duty and remind my confronter and the other protesters that although they were permitted to display their corpses on university property, they could not block access to or egress from my building. Then I nervously rattled off a few of the policies that came to mind:

"Students have a right to assemble."

Pause.

"Free speech is honored on our campus."

Pause.

"Other students have the right to gather to learn about bona fide employment opportunities."

Pause.

More administrivia. "Blah, blah, blah."

Boom! There it was. I was officially an "administrator," a soulless bureaucratic-sounding label I never thought would describe me. Worse yet, it occurred to me that I was part of the phenomenon of administrative bloat, a campus "suit" whose day-to-day was filled with, well, administrivia. I am sure to the student I came across as nothing more than Charlie's Brown's squawking school teacher from my *Peanuts* cartoons as a kid. I was uttering noise that did nothing to create understanding.

Gone were the days when I played the ever-so-hip campus staffer, bonding with students while reminding them that actually I wasn't all that much older than they were. I used to get them, I thought. Today, though, I was a middle-aged director, old enough to be this protester's father. I was a "unit head" on the vice chancellor's org chart, or an MSP (management services professional) for payroll purposes. Today, I—the suit, administrator, unit head, and MSP—didn't "get them" at all.

The evening progressed with a packed house of eager students soaking up insight from our CIA guests. The dozen protesters silently held large handwritten signs in the back of the room, holding them high over their heads. On one I read, WHY DO YOU MURDER INNOCENT PEOPLE? Another said, IS TORTURE PART OF YOUR AGENCY'S MISSION STATEMENT?

Eventually, the information session ended, and I guided the recruiters down a hallway to the back door of the building, where I had a car waiting to take them safely to their vehicles in a perimeter parking garage.

Driving home that night I thought, *Maybe that student was right. Maybe I did need to discover my moral compass.*

THE ADMINISTRATOR'S PURPOSE PROBLEM

If you pay close attention to administrative leaders on your campus whose tone you admire—a tone that demonstrates control, comfort, energy, steadiness, and optimism—chances are they have clarified and aligned their values, that internal navigation system that says, "This is who I am when I am at my best." It's one thing to explore sources of engagement on your campus as I described in the last chapter. It's quite another to fully understand how your role on that campus adds meaning to your life, let alone to beam out that meaning for your colleagues and students to absorb.

The tone setters around you are worth watching; they somehow wear their values on their sleeve. Their North Star shines brightly. What they have in abundance is a laser focus on institutional mission and how the individual "purpose" they walk underscores that mission. Richard Leider, best-selling author of *The Power of Purpose*, writes "I can often tell when I'm with a person who has unlocked their purpose in life or is doing purpose projects that light them up. They have a curiosity and an energy about them that draws me in and lights me up."

But how do we achieve that? For most of the clients I coach, the very idea of defining their purpose reads too hippie-dippie. As one humorously described it, "It brings on a psychic rash of purpose anxiety." I can relate. It's too heady a concept for us to lock into our reality, as if trying to embody a cheesy tagline from our school's admissions brochure. Trying to concoct a crisp purpose statement makes me feel too one-dimensional, too commoditized for the human marketplace. I feel that I am more than that. You may feel the same way. Instead, some of my clients end up rattling off platitudes like "My purpose is to be of service" or to "make an impact" or to "care for my family." Any of these are reasonable expressions of purpose but only if the words have juice. After all, what does service really mean? How can you be sure you are making an impact? What exactly does it look like when you have achieved care for your family?

As Pablo Picasso mused, "The meaning of life is to find your gift. The purpose of life is to give it away." My father, the college professor and minister, embraced that sentiment with clear-eyed clarity. He lived a life of service to his God and to humanity—full stop. In part, he is the inspiration for this book. Dad lived the magnificence of his authentic purpose, defined as a stable and generalized intention to accomplish something that is at the same time meaningful to the self and consequential for the world beyond the self. I have always envied that—this ability to find a purpose that boldly feeds our selfishness while at the same time making an impact far beyond ourselves, the ultimate win-win.

Realtors can find purpose. So can bankers, engineers, hotel workers, and bill collectors. The director of parking and transportation services on your own campus can claim their purpose, and I give that administrator props for leading what is the most thankless office in higher education history next to the bursar! Surely, we can get there too.

If only I were clear on my purpose, maybe I would have landed a crisper response to the scruffy UCSD student agitator who asked me to find my moral compass.

IF ONLY WE WERE FACULTY

For my father and the legions of teaching and research faculty on our campuses, the question of purpose might generate a quizzical look in their eyes and a condescending response. "What a silly question," they might say. They have connected to a very specific intellectual pursuit—whether it be arts, humanities, sciences, business, engineering, or the growing number of hybrid disciplines. If they pursue tenure track roles, their path is clear though far from easy. From the rank of assistant professor to associate professor and the stabilizing job guarantee of the ultimate—a full professorship—our academic partners' agendas are tracked and monitored. As they rise in their hierarchy, they must teach, publish, and secure grant money. Often they must also train and mentor graduate students, those whom they hope will follow them on their purpose path. Faculty are seldom well versed in the overall campus operation or the ultimate student experience. Their portfolios are highly specialized, and their purpose is dialed into a specific intellectual problem that they, and only they (plus maybe a team of researchers), can hope to solve.

For those of us staffing the administrative ranks, it's harder to hit such an evolved bullseye. Our jobs don't copy and paste neatly onto a course syllabus. Any add-ons we commit to—whether teaching a class, serving on a committee, working the phones for the annual giving campaign, lining students up at commencement, or volunteering to help families unpack their minivans during move-in—such growth opportunities rarely come with release time or additional compensation for us.

46

They don't populate a compelling tenure packet—we don't have one. And our summers can be as busy as our falls, winters, and springs. Our families, who claim to be impressed by our higher education careers but have no understanding of how we spend our time, will say, much to our annoyance, "You are so lucky to have summers off." Actually, most of us are on twelve-month appointments, and we don't enjoy guaranteed sabbaticals after five years, do we?

It is tough to find purpose within the frenzy of so much administrative tasking. True, if you are in admissions, you can analyze the competitiveness of your entering class. If you are in academic support, you can pour over retention data. Advancement jobs connect to progress on the latest capital campaign. Athletics' coaches can fixate on team wins and promising freshman recruits. Quantifying our work can give us a purpose bump, but it's often fleeting. Pure metrics lose their sex appeal if there isn't a driver bigger than the numbers. Faculty will almost always have their academic discipline to fall back on, and once they have reached full tenure, they'll have tremendous flexibility to deepen their intellectual commitment to what matters most to them. Our path is different.

PASSION IS DIFFICULT

So much staff energy is expended helping students declare majors and helping them find that spark within that is so all-encompassing they must pursue it. Confucius once said, "Choose a job you love and you will never have to work a day in your life." Although the quote sings—and let's be honest, many of us have probably used it on students whose majors are undeclared—it creates life expectations that are impossible to realize. University of Pennsylvania Wharton professor and best-selling author Adam Grant writes, "Following your passion is a luxury. Following your values is a necessity. Passion is a fickle magnet: it pulls you toward your current interests. Values are a steady compass: they point you toward a future purpose." Grant adds, "Passion brings immediate joy. Values provide lasting meaning." Now we are getting somewhere. If only there were a model.

In 2022, we lost a great writer and theologian when Frederick Buechner passed away. Perhaps his most famous quote, often bandied about on faith-based campuses to study the essence of purpose, went like this: "Your vocation in life comes from where your greatest joy meets the world's greatest need." Buechner's point was that whatever we choose to do, in whatever profession and industry, we owe it to ourselves to pursue a career that feels more like a vocation than a day job. That's how I felt in my early university career when I met all those tone setters who exuded this authentic calling to their work.

Taken a step further, Buechner's vocation has been expanded to the inspirational world of blue zones, areas around the globe with a higher-than-normal percentage of residents enjoying healthy lives beyond a hundred years of age. The most famous example is the island of Okinawa, which has more centenarians than any other place in the world. These Japanese elders argue that all of us have what's called an *ikigai*, loosely translated to our "reason for being," our raison d'être. According to proponents of *ikigai*, finding our purpose is the job of our lifetimes. It's more about pursuit than about arrival. As university administrators, for you and I to hit our *ikigai* bullseye as campus tone setters, we must answer yes to these questions:

- Do you love what you are doing (at least most of the time)?
- Are you skilled at what you are doing?
- Is there an institutional need for what you are doing?
- Can you be paid a reasonable wage for what you are doing?

OK. Let's be honest. We don't meet many people in life, including our campus tone setters, who answer with a resounding "Yes and a-men!" as they raise their hands to the heavens as if at a gospel revival. Rather, tone setters are apt to play with the *ikigai* framework, making sometimes minor adjustments to make the transition from job (little "j") to Vocation (capital "V").

For example, if you are underwhelmed by your position description but like to play games, you can treat your role as a puzzle, looking for places of inefficiency and creating streamlined processes. If you are feeling in over your head and lack the skill to be optimally effective, pursuing free and low-cost professional development options will build confidence and boost your credibility. If you feel that your department is not directly meeting a student or institutional need, you can become more strategic and utilize assessment metrics to develop an ironclad link between articulated campus needs and the work you do. And if you are not paid well, you can consider other roles either on your current campus or elsewhere. In truth, if salary is your weakest *ikigai* component, you'll be better served by pursuing roles elsewhere. Once you are in a particular college or university HR system, your increases become incremental and are rarely substantial. As a client of mine shared in a recent coaching conversation, "I feel like I am doing the work of two people. I can't understand why they won't double my salary." I gently reminded him that this is not going to happen; it almost never does.

VALUES CONSTELLATION

For most of us, we need an easier path to purpose, a framework we can make our own. This is where tone setters' values come in—the words, phrases, and expressions they can readily articulate that represent who they are when they are at their best. When I coach administrative leaders, we spend a great deal of time developing what I refer to as their values constellation. This may be a bulleted list in Microsoft Word, an Excel spreadsheet, an infographic, or even for some a vibrant vision board—all this so that they land the exact descriptive language to express what they stand for. It's my way of helping them sneak into the most daunting task of self-reflection, their purpose. By naming the values that spotlight our best and most authentic selves, we can start to gather data on our higher education experience to better understand what works, what doesn't, and how we might make some modifications to bring our values into resonance.

For instance, if one of your values is *creativity*, I as your coach will ask you what *creativity* means to you. How do you know when you are being creative? What's the proof? When you go to sleep each night, can you reflect on your day and point to experiences where *creativity* was activated? And what if you had a bad day with this value? What if *creativity* was absent, stepped on, or ignored?

When I was completing my training as a coach, my certification supervisor would drill my values. Here's how it went with my value of *impact*.

"What do you mean by the word *impact*, Andy? You say that's one of your values, but I don't really know what that means. Can you tell me about it?"

He continued. "How do you know when you have activated that value?"

He went on. "On a scale of one to ten, with one being clunky dissonance and ten being solid resonance, where would you rank yourself on the value of *impact*?"

He wasn't done yet: "What can you do to further amplify your *impact*?"

"Are you paying attention to your *impact* every day, Andy?"

Geez, Louise! I thought. *It's just a damn word.*

And there is the rub. *Impact* is a word that I claim represents who I am when I am highly functioning, fulfilled, and crystal clear. Along with my other values, it's my map of an area that should be largely within my grasp. While I may not have much control over the latest reorganization that changed my role or the agenda of my new president or the budget cuts that came after a drop in student enrollment, I should have agency over what makes me tick, what drives me, what gets me in my flow.

Our values are ours to create, cultivate, and fully express. And when your morale as a college tone setter takes a dip, and it will, you can point to the value that is being minimized, ignored, or stepped on. Then you can develop a strategy to enliven it. It's yours to resuscitate. This is the antithesis of helplessness. This is you in the driver's seat. Your campus will surely put your constellation of values to the test. Perhaps it already has.

My client on a university marketing team ignited her value of *collaboration* by building a campus-wide network of communicators from the various colleges and schools. Another student life director I coached activated his value of *compassion* by spending extra time during the COVID-19 shutdown to drop care packages off at the doors of his staff members, ringing and running so as not to put members of his team at risk. My associate director client in a study abroad office described a strong value around *sustainability* and took the lead on establishing a practice of ensuring her university was educating students about their carbon footprint before sending them offshore. Even I, with a value of *vibrant aesthetics*, was able to find myself in leadership roles for four extensive office renovations in my career. For any of these clients and for me, none of our values were articulated in our position descriptions. Rather, each of us found ways to fill gaps on our campuses while at the same time living our values.

Here I provide three examples of values constellations from higher education clients. Look at how differently each client articulates their constellation.

EXAMPLE 1

I value *flow*.
- Integrated life of well-distributed activities—space, liberation, simplicity, and moving fluidly among mind, body, and spirit with optimism, momentum, and purpose.
- Accountability (being "on it")—on time, responsive, in sync with what surrounds me, or better yet, a step ahead.
- Equanimity—appropriate responsiveness through highs and lows.
- Balanced technology—technology that streamlines and enriches.

I value *influence*.
- Proven impact—helping people discover and implement their authentic contribution in the midst of opportunity, disruption, stagnation, or disillusionment.
- Reputable voice—as demonstrated by opportunities to speak, facilitate, write, and consult effortlessly.

I value *connection* and *presence*.
- Meaningful interactions—with friends, family, collaborators, clients, and others whose paths I cross.
- Belonging—comfort in a variety of settings, regardless of role or level of control.
- Self-awareness—prioritizing opportunities to be present with myself.

I value *awe*.

- Vibrant aesthetics—color, light, space (reflected at home, in possessions, and through my professional identity).
- Intentional pause—appreciation in the moment for what is beautiful, interesting, resonant, and even discordant.
- Abundant spirituality—awesomeness of individual and collective power.

EXAMPLE 2

- Everything is everything. Making one small thing better in one place makes everything else a little better too.
- People over products. The most important thing in a project are the people involved.
- There's always tomorrow. Nothing is ever done. Problems can be solved. Projects can be renewed. Everything is in a state of becoming.
- Take care of the small things, and the large things will fall into place.
- Kindness and generosity beget virtuous cycles of improvement.

EXAMPLE 3

"When I am at my best, I am a *curious* thinker who actively seeks out other points of view and keeps an open mind. I recognize that there are two sides to every coin and that no problem is as easy to solve as it first appears. I am a *creative* problem solver and an effective *storyteller* with an active imagination. I am committed to my *duty* for preserving and protecting the planet and its most vulnerable inhabitants, and I act from a place of *empathy* and understanding toward others. I strive to act honestly and selflessly and to hold myself and others to a high standard of personal *integrity*."

Perhaps Gandhi provides our most articulate expression of the importance of defining our values.

Keep your thoughts positive because your thoughts become your WORDS.

Keep your words positive because your words become your BEHAVIOR.

Keep your behavior positive because your behavior becomes your HABITS.

Keep your habits positive because your habits become your VALUES.

Keep your values positive because your values become your DESTINY.

TONE SETTER MINDSETS

As you slide into your purpose and assess how your higher education career fuels that purpose, I encourage you to develop and practice purpose habits. Tone setters do their jobs, and they somehow make those jobs richer than they would otherwise be. They breathe in the energy from their work and from their lives, and they exhale in a manner that makes things better.

MINDSET #12

Develop and maintain your values constellation.
The creation of your constellation of values should be much more than another coaching exercise. It can start as simply as a Google search for the word "values." Select no more than five words, and commit them to memory. Think about them each day. Play with the order and the phrasing. Let your constellation marinate and shift until you have landed on something that can stand the test of time. I conduct a values check at the end of every quarter each year, stepping away from my day-to-day to an inspired place that is not part of my routine (i.e., a beautiful park, a garden, a cozy coffee shop). I pause with each value, ranking each one from one to ten (one being "no resonance" and ten being "strong resonance"). I spend time with the values that score less than five, considering what actions I might take in the next three months to activate those values. I also determine if I need to edit the values, perhaps adding a new one or deleting one that no longer represents my true self.

Mindset #13

Cultivate your wisdom portfolio.

I have noticed that as we mature in our administrative roles, we become wiser and better able to digest the results of the various self-assessment exercises we complete in our careers. Tools like MBTI, DISC, Strong, Enneagram, StrengthsFinder, Hogan, and others tell a story about our behaviors and priorities and the impressions we make on others. They provide data points, and over time we can more readily see the connections between them and the visible theme of self they showcase. Self-assessment instruments measure our inclinations, good and bad, and should be a part of what I call our wisdom portfolio (WP), essentially a gathering place of our documented tone over the course of our lives. Some of my clients use an old shoe box for their WP. For others it's a dog-eared file tucked away in a cabinet at home. For the more tech savvy, their WP is an electronic folder on their desktop, tablet, or smartphone. Whatever storage system you choose, your WP should contain all these representations of you in growth mode. Some administrators include journals they keep, presentations they are proud of, performance appraisals, and even cards and letters from students reminding them of the positive tone they set.

Mindset #14

Update your résumé and socials.

All this work we do on values and on purpose can be validated with a strong social media presence—on X, Instagram, Facebook, and most of all on LinkedIn. When people Google us (and by the way, we should Google ourselves from time to time), they will be directed to whatever we have chosen to curate online. I have worked with higher education clients who have attempted job searches with outdated or typo-ridden LinkedIn profiles or with old or inappropriate head shots or banners. As I gently remind them, if you have chosen to develop a social media profile, then you need to either be accountable for it or delete it. Your profile should be up-to-date and ready for prime time. The same is true for your résumé, CV, and biography. This is not just about looking for the next job. Socials, résumé, and bio updates are an important component to telling your story and ensuring a story that is accurate and in alignment with your values. Make a point of updating all of these on a calendared basis that makes sense for you.

Mindset #15

Develop an annual report.

I'll write that again. Develop an annual report. Why would you do that, especially if your boss didn't ask you? Looking at your personal and organization's accomplishments each year can be an important engagement milestone. It lets you keep track and officially monitor the efforts that are flourishing and those that may be diminishing. Your report doesn't need to be long or professionally designed. It represents a year in the life, and it becomes a treasured time capsule for you and anyone who succeeds you.

Mindset #16

Pursue growth opportunities that fuel your purpose.

As we live our values and monitor them so that we know which ones need activation, we may also find ourselves doing more than is required—that's a good thing. Consider expressing interest in joining search committees for open positions, reading admission files during the selection cycle, or volunteering for homecoming weekend. Or you might beta test new budget technologies or assist the development office with the Annual Day of Giving. These can be optimal ways to leverage your campus ecosystem to create interesting side hustles, not for money (necessarily) but out of curiosity, a desire to grow, and a savvy way of awakening sleeping values.

MINDSET #17

Expand your perspective beyond your campus bubble.

It can become too easy for our campus to consume us. We can eat in the dining hall. We can work out in the gym. We may be able to drop our kids off at campus daycare. We can earn an additional degree, take a class on Excel pivot tables, and meet with a financial adviser. Be sure you know when it is time to go home. Keep your campus life fresh by feeding your values outside your higher education career. Fuel your interest in writing poetry, renovating your house, coaching sports, or losing yourself in a transformative vacation. The freshness you demonstrate on campus is in direct correlation to the freshness you curate beyond the campus. Your campus role is a part of who you are. It is not all that you are.

MINDSET #18

Become a data geek.

What are your enrollment targets, retention numbers, and capital campaign milestones? How many students attend your programs and from what majors? Assessment and big data have arrived on campus (finally!), and they are here to stay, regardless of your role. Even the most qualitative of jobs has a set of key performance indicators (KPIs). Know the KPIs that relate to your area of responsibility. What's growing? What's constricting? What's untouched and needing attention?

POWERFUL QUESTION

What actions can you take to create alignment between your values and your university role?

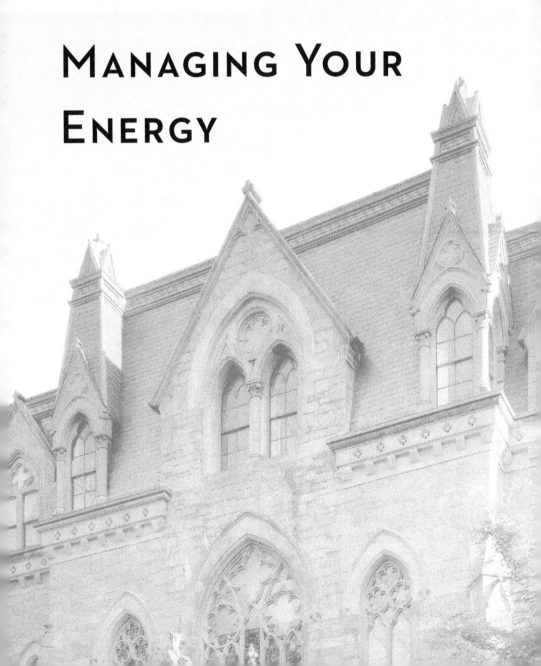

PART TWO

MANAGING YOUR ENERGY

FOR UNIVERSITY ADMINISTRATORS today, it's all too easy to lose track of time, undervalue our professional relationships, and ignore the beauty of our physical surroundings on campus. We can either find ways to sustain and renew our energy, or we can feel the drain as it depletes. The choice is ours.

I often talk with my clients about energy—where it comes from, how to hold onto it, and what to do when it is lost. Look at it this way: your energy is like the charge meter on your smartphone. It drops to 0 percent if you don't plug it in. And when the screen goes dark, it can feel like a crisis. That's why many of us have phone charging stations throughout our environments—on our bedside tables, at our kitchen countertops, and in our cars, where we can feel the comfort of a rising charge—10 percent, 30 percent, 50 percent, 75 percent, 100 percent! Phew!

To be a tone setter, you need to creatively manage your energy. You need to learn when and where to generate it and toward what to direct it. You need to know when your energy has been exhausted and it is time to rest and recharge.

How do we set our tone with an energy charge that remains consistently much closer to 100 percent than to 0 percent? As we will explore in the next three chapters, our relationship with time, with people, and with our built environment provides needed insight into how we can best manage our energy on a college campus.

CHAPTER 4

TIME

Value the Moments

Time passes whether I stand still or move.

—Anne Barngrover

A S WE NOTICE the tone setters on our campuses, we recognize that their impact is rarely the result of overextended calendars. As we know, higher education is notorious for meetings, lots of them. But between the busyness of meetings and many other commitments to be some place at some time, tone setters carve out the rejuvenation space in between the hustle of their days. According to London's School of Life, "It might be that the real threat to our happiness and self-development lies not in our failure to be busy, but in the opposite scenario: our inability to be 'lazy' enough." Tone setters effectively reframe their relationship with time in order to optimize their campus experiences. Here are some questions I'd like you to ponder:

- Are you often feeling harried on campus?
- Do you have a tendency to overschedule?
- Do you rush into meetings late or leave early?
- Is your smartphone a constant distraction?
- Are you multitasking during Zoom calls?

Santa Clara University

For many years I was *that* administrator. You know the one. I would grab a prewrapped sandwich in the dining hall's food court and eat it at my desk while I managed the deluge in my email inbox. That was until I met Mitch Joslin at Santa Clara University, who invited me to a midday workout at the recently opened Malley Fitness Center on campus. I eagerly accepted.

Santa Clara University is the oldest college in California and the site of one of the state's original Catholic Missions. Once part of the sprawling fruit orchards that comprised the Valley of the Heart's Delight, today's Santa Clara sits in the midst of Silicon Valley behemoths—Applied Materials, Lockheed Martin, Apple, and many others are within a short drive along El Camino Real, the meandering Kings Highway that connects the Bay Area's South Bay to the area's most famous city, San Francisco.

Santa Clara is private, and it's also Jesuit, known for many things, from its holistic social justice underpinnings to its exquisite Mission-style campus, where even the trash bins match the tile rooftops of the surrounding buildings. Once considered a regional university, Santa Clara has successfully broadened its admissions reach to include "rain birds" from Pacific Northwest private and public high schools and Hawaiian students trading in their island fever for a mainland college experience. The university's rigorous academic programs have launched thousands of successful careers in business, law, engineering, education, and nonprofit management. Gavin Newsom, Leon Panetta, Janet Napolitano, and Brandi Chastain famously attended Santa Clara.

Though my directorship at SCU was a solid one, the move to Silicon Valley was less about my career mobility than a promising future for my beloved, Skip, who had also found a professional home base in campus administration. He was pursuing a tremendous opportunity in Santa Clara's School of Law, and it just so happened that there was an opening at the same time in the university's centralized Career Center. Both job listings appeared in the *Chronicle of Higher Education* the same week. Skip applied for his desired job, and I applied for mine.

As if by divine providence, Skip and I were both invited for campus interviews on the very same day. Except for a very few insiders, no one knew the two of us were finalists for similar directorships on opposite sides of campus from one another. There the two of us sat in the university's see-and-be-seen dining room in the historic Adobe Lodge, Skip on one side lunching with his search committee and me on the other with mine. Other than a wink and a grin to each other across the crowded space, we each focused our attention on our respective audiences. It was surreal. Both of us were extended offers within a week.

We were the first gay couple hired concurrently in the university's long history. As we said farewell to our colleagues at our previous university, University of Texas at Austin, some expressed concerns that a faith-based university may not be a welcoming place for the two of us. In fact, Skip and I have worked concurrently at four universities. Nowhere did we feel more welcomed and supported as individuals and as a couple than at Santa Clara. And nowhere did I enjoy campus events more than when I was nibbling on cheese and crackers and sipping the university's own labeled Chardonnay with the parents of incoming freshmen. Chilled California Chardonnay is my go-to refresher to this day.

Time was filled with gratitude.

When Mitch met me in the gym one fall day at noon, I was happy to establish a healthy habit at my new campus home. Mitch was an experienced student affairs colleague, having served previously at schools like UC Santa Barbara, Montana State, Temple, and Azusa Pacific before landing at SCU as an adviser to various student leadership groups. He was muscled and fit—he still is to this day—and he knew his way around a weight room. I had always been an avid evening walker, but my midlife administrator's waistline called for more than a renewal of my WeightWatchers membership. And I was ready to do what had never occurred to me before—to break up my busy day with self-care. For three days a week over the course of several months, Mitch gave up his lunch hour to serve as my trainer. He taught me body-boosting techniques like lat pulls, cable rows, biceps curls, triceps kickbacks, dumbbell shoulder presses, and of course treadmill and elliptical protocols. Under his watchful eye, I worked all the muscle groups—shoulders, back, chest, legs, and core.

I was using work time in a new way, and once I overcame some productivity guilt, it felt good, and my afternoons became more energized.

Time was in my control.

My Santa Clara experience also taught me how precious time is. It felt like the entire campus community filled the pews at the university's historic Mission Church. Hundreds of us—students, faculty, and staff—were summoned there by President Father Locatelli to reflect, pray, hug, sing, and try to gain some understanding of the unthinkable tragedies that had taken place hours before in Pennsylvania, Virginia, and New York. It was September 11, 2001. At that moment, my mind was fixated not on my career but on the magic that transformed a cluster of buildings and grassy quads to a place of ritual, growth, and belonging. There was no place I would rather have been on that day and no better way to experience time. We later learned that one of our sophomores was among those who perished in that tragedy.

Time stood still.

OUR RELATIONSHIP WITH TIME

You and I are operating within the same twenty-four-hour cycle as our early riser campus landscapers, our sleep-deprived students, our successful alumni, and our overextended college presidents. But how can we get playful with our calendar and orchestrate our time rather than fighting against it? For tone setters, time is an effortless flow, not a battle to the finish.

Here are some things I've heard from clients:

> "You don't understand! Fiscal close consumes me for the entire month of July."
> "Getting payroll processed takes all of my time."
> "Summer orientation? It's totally wild!"
> "I barely have time to breathe during the first two weeks of the fall semester."

"When I am doing annual performance appraisals, I don't have time for anything else."

"Are you kidding? This week is dorm move-in! No, I can't possibly attend your meeting."

"I keep my out-of-office message on all the time—there is no way I can keep up with all the email."

"We're about to launch the public phase of the Capital Campaign. I'm swamped!"

Perhaps part of our challenge in higher education is that its cycles create sometimes overwhelming busyness spikes and less rigorous swaths of free time (though few I know would admit to the latter). Tone setters manage to level the load, moving through time as if it were endless. There is an ease and a flow to their energy.

When asked, "How are you?" is your response too frequently, "I am so busy!"?

The Resilience Institute refers to such sentiments as the makings of "grindset," a negative counter to the positive mindsets I offer throughout this book. Admittedly, throughout my career I can recall more occasions than I care to admit where a public display of grindset was my operating mode. It somehow felt righteous to give the appearance of a whirling dervish to others. It was socially acceptable campus parlance and a not-so-subtle suggestion that I was accomplishing more than mere mortals. Of course, my expression of busyness would often generate a nod from my questioner and sometimes a one-up, like "Busy? Let me tell you about busy—my world is insane right now!" I always found this to be a vacuous exchange. Truthfully, I was never convincing at playing the overwhelmed staff member. The ultimate J on the Myers Briggs scale, I was all about plans and structures and systems to prevent the likelihood that I would become overwhelmed. I pulled an all-nighter in college, just once, because I thought that's what one did. And as I dragged myself, half-asleep through the next day of classes, I remember thinking, *What a ridiculous waste of time.*

Tone setters don't create space for grindset theater. When you and I are in the presence of a campus tone setter, we feel seen, heard, respected, and fully engaged, despite the busyness of their day and the stressors they carry that we can't begin to fathom. They don't check their phones as if by nervous tick. For at this particular moment, they generously grant us their time and their attention. They are present with us. And they don't expend oxygen by telling us how overextended they are.

Time was a gift.

Are You in a Rush?

My years at Santa Clara were not without existential struggle. Much of my energy was spent trying to figure out how to make an impact, who to know and who I thought should know me, and how to uber-busy myself. I felt like the clock was ticking. This marked my third administrative role, and it was finally dawning on me that my time was largely my own. My boss was a kind and supportive religious studies professor named Dr. Philip Riley who went by the adorable name Boo. Aside from my standing meetings with him, my "Boo time" as I called it, I was free to innovate by developing new high-impact programs, crafting new position descriptions for my staff, and broadening our center's communication throughout all schools and departments.

I learned that the gift of freedom comes at a cost, especially for administrators like me looking for some direction from above. High-level strategy didn't come in this case, and I found that stressful. I've since learned that what I was experiencing was a good kind of stress, one that was healthy and kept me on the edge of my creativity. There is actually a name for such good stress. It is called eustress, a combination of the Greek prefix "eu," meaning "good," with the English word stress, and it was introduced by Hans Selye in 1976 to define our responses to stressors that lead to the positive outcomes of meaning, hope, and vigor.

Time was mine to invent.

Upon reflection, my time at Santa Clara presented a bountiful resource—a resource I utilized, spent, tracked, saved for, and ultimately valued years later in the rearview mirror. I remember seeing the provost walking alone through the campus Mission Gardens each morning, the fragrance of wisteria all around. She moved slowly, with her head bowed as if in prayer. There was nothing in her hands; they were clasped in front of her. As I rushed by her, briefcase in one hand and a grande Peet's coffee in the other, eager to be the first in my office to get a jump start on the day, it was clear that this was not a perky "Good morning, Provost!" moment. The provost was experiencing time in her own ritualistic way, and me in mine. As she mindfully equipped herself for her day, I leaped head-on into mine.

Although higher education practitioners aren't the only professionals who struggle with time, for so many of my clients today, the topic of time management ranks high on their list of coaching goals they hope to master. For them, and perhaps for you, they desire more than platitudes like how to "work smarter and not harder." So many of them are adding value to their campus communities while living complex lives off campus—raising families, caring for elders, completing additional degrees, and serving their communities. It seems that every minute matters, and the worst way to end a day on campus is to feel that their time has not been effectively utilized.

FINDING YOUR TIME STYLE

Your relationship with time is just that: *your* relationship with time. It is yours to customize to suit your tone. For instance, a former law school dean to whom Skip reported was revered by all as a highly organized and deeply compassionate leader. Skip used to marvel at how she would run her weekly management team meetings. There Skip and six of his colleagues sat, around the conference table, and at five minutes before the top of the hour when the meeting was scheduled to end, the dean would pause, smile, look around the table, and in a single motion close her padfolio and stand up, signifying the end of the meeting. Skip and his colleagues knew that the time had come and would rise on cue, say their goodbyes, and clear the dean's office so that she and they could prepare for her next commitment. Skip's dean set a clear tone about time, and her direct reports honored that tone.

A friend once told me, "A good job doesn't love you back." I never quite bought that. For me, it implied that my work was in no way a creative contribution, that it was merely a series of tasks in exchange for a monthly paycheck. I've learned from college and university tone setters that the time we spend on our campuses should be about much more than money in exchange of services. Emeritus Vice Chancellor of Student Affairs at UCLA Janina Montero is known to say, *"El trabajo dignifica,"* which loosely translates to "Work dignifies." There is a way in which we carry ourselves, physically and emotionally, that somehow shows that we are in the right place *at the right time* and doing the right thing.

TONE SETTER MINDSETS

Authors Richard Leider and Rich Feller once quipped, "Some people burn out and others rust out." Neither are good options. Redefining your relationship with time will alleviate stress and enable you to set and experience a tone in full alignment with your values and purpose. Tone setters curate their time. They sculpt time. They reinvent time. They create space to simply pass the time. Our higher education careers afford us endless opportunities to make peace with time.

MINDSET #19

Check your busyness vocabulary.

Reconsider your public talk about time. If you instill a sense of being overwhelmed to others (even if you are doing so with the best of intentions), you create a deficit perception that becomes a reality. Cut pandering statements from your discourse that only amplify people's anxiety about time, such as "I know we all are super busy" or "It will be so nice when the semester ends so we can relax." Rather, focus your discourse on effort, progress, and culmination. As Zen master and consultant Marc Lesser offers, "When you're stressed by too many obligations, you might say, 'I'm juggling a lot of plates.' But what if you reframed that as, 'I'm planting lots of seeds.' Not only is the analogy more calming (gardening versus juggling), it evokes a different expectation: not the pessimistic idea that some plates will inevitably fall and shatter, but the hope that some seeds will invariably germinate and grow." These may be merely words, but our words create perceptions.

MINDSET #20
Adopt an 80-20 "good enough" rule.

Each and every task matters, but each and every task does not matter to the same extent. This is hard for many of my clients to digest. Higher education leaders who seek coaching are typically driven and accomplished contributors. They take pride in doing everything well and struggle with the inevitable reality that sometimes good enough simply needs to be good enough. A simple hack popularized by the Positive Intelligence work of Shirzad Chamine is to break up your administrative workload into effort that is of greatest impact and spend 80 percent of your time on that. Spend only 20 percent of your time on administrivia and other must-do actions that though necessary are of lesser importance. This feeds your achievement desire while placing your intellectual and creative energy in areas of primary importance. As Voltaire once proclaimed, "Perfect is the enemy of good." Let's focus on delivering *good* and gently aspire to *perfect*.

MINDSET #21
Schedule heavy lifting at personally optimal times.

Each of us recharges in different ways, and each of us has times when we are the most prone to experience flow. Schedule efforts that require thought and concentration when your energy for this kind of work is optimal. It's important that we not treat every hour of our day on campus equally. For some, early morning provides a good time to get caught up and set the stage for the day. For others, Friday afternoons when energy may be low are a great time to clean up the week, organizing the email inbox and checking the calendar for the following week. Find a rhythm that works for you so that you honor the peaks and valleys of your energy. We all have them.

MINDSET #22

Develop a foolproof calendaring system.

I have long been an advocate of calendar management. One of the best ways to enhance our relationship with time is by utilizing a calendaring system that organizes and honors time. Whether Outlook, Google, or an old-fashioned daily planner, the tools available to us make it easy to feel a reasonable sense of control over our time. For me, color is important, and I colorize events to give me a visual on how my time is spent: blue for meetings, yellow for exercise and wellness, green for coaching appointments, red for volunteer activities, and so forth. I have also become crafty at scheduling buffers, creating space between commitments. For instance, my client coaching appointments are forty-five minutes, providing me fifteen minutes after each to summarize my notes, stretch, and prepare for the next session. I also build in travel time between commitments so that I am never rushed.

MINDSET #23

Create space for nothing.

In the words of Lin Yutang, "The wisdom of life consists of the elimination of non-essentials." Some call this deep time. In my Google calendar, there are blocks each day I call *Flow*. It is those unscheduled blocks where our minds can rest and wander and often surprise us with innovation, optimism, and clarity. One of the hardest things to do when bolstering our relationship with time is to embrace free time when there is nothing planned. So, if you need to block time on your calendar and call it *Play*, then do it. A former boss of mine scheduled what she called *Magic Time*. It's rare that we accomplish everything we intend. Stuff happens. Move items on your calendar or set reminders to free your mind of things left undone.

Mindset #24

Complement your work with outside interests.

We all end up making time for what we cherish. Work hard, sure. But play hard too, ensuring that you are developing your interests outside your higher education identity. Get curious about the campus tone setters who post pictures of their kids' milestones or never miss a weekly yoga class or play in a pickleball league or create time to take up painting. They are fueling a full life that honors the value they place in their campus work while expanding in other areas of personal importance. Focus on a full life rather than a busy work life.

Mindset #25

Lighten your commuting baggage.

We can get a sense of people's management of time with how much stuff they cart home with them. I call this our "files of good intentions." The good news is that fewer of us are carrying heavy binders around with us. On those days when you are on campus, consider being as hands-free as possible when you come and go, maybe carrying only one bag or backpack. This can be surprisingly liberating. It makes you lighter, and it demonstrates a liberation in your relationship with time. You are not bogged down. You are free.

POWERFUL QUESTION

What would your campus career look like if time were plentiful?

CHAPTER 5

PEOPLE
EMBRACE THE RELATIONSHIPS

*There is a famous dialogue from the Zen tradition where
the student asks the teacher, "What is the teaching
of a lifetime?"*
The teacher replies, "An appropriate response."
—MARC LESSER

I T DOESN'T MATTER if you are a university president or have a job several boxes below on the org chart. The tone you set with all the people in your sphere—those you lead, those you support, and those with whom you collaborate to do your job—is a huge determinant of your success and satisfaction as a campus administrator.

In my experience as an executive coach, most of my clients focus our sessions on what I'll call people problems. And in a way, this is not surprising. When most of us enter the academy as staff members, we arrive with high expectations of the human relationships our work will afford us. Maybe a career in university administration will be like our halcyon college days—our former campus life of tight friendships, entertaining distractions, clear guidance (a syllabus), and regular performance appraisals (grades). Perhaps in our staff roles there will be a lockstep progression, just like when we were undergraduates. We think that our professional milestones will be clear and that there will be a lot of institutional energy directed toward our ultimate success (graduation). Our key milestones are always just a semester or two away.

College administration will be the best time in our life, relived, right? Not necessarily. Such nostalgia can create a wide gap between our expectations of human behavior and the ultimate and inevitable reality of our human interactions as paid staff members. Underneath all the academic regalia and institutional ritual are people. They are flawed. So are we. Their judgment is subjective, as is ours. "The hardest part is the human part," says one of the slogans developed by cultural design group Gapingvoid, whose bright, whimsical posters fill lobbies and hallways on many campuses today.

We didn't choose corporate careers to begin with. Or perhaps we pivoted from corporate careers. But regardless, our campuses never provide refuge from people problems. Indeed, they include all the peculiarities of any other industry, perhaps even more because of our two-category structure: faculty and staff, each with its own procedures and processes. In higher education, we trade stockholders for boards of regents, high-flying executives for fussy parents, and quirky engineers for bigger-than-life college presidents. The paradox for so many of us, and for the tone setters who offer us inspiration, is that it is in fact people who present our biggest challenge and our greatest opportunity.

UNIVERSITY OF PENNSYLVANIA

The May sunshine peeked brightly through the trees on the shady West Philadelphia campus, and its main pedestrian thoroughfare, Locust Walk, was alive with bright smiles and Instagram photo-ops as graduating seniors donned their newly purchased gowns and caps. Laughter filled the air as students debated which side of their mortar boards the tassel should dangle from. I took it in as I stood beside the statue of bespectacled and erudite University of Pennsylvania founder Benjamin Franklin sitting on his bench as if he were absorbing the scene along with me. This was the first opportunity in two years that students had an in-person graduation to anticipate—such milestones were shuttered due to the COVID-19 pandemic.

Locust Walk is Penn's primary thoroughfare, lined on either side by an eclectic mix of historic townhomes and classroom buildings. From this vantage point, it is hard to imagine that Penn is an urban campus, tucked in the heart of Philadelphia's University City neighborhood, couched mostly between one-way Walnut Street as it flows into Center City and Chestnut Street as it heads toward the western suburbs. Founded in 1740, Penn is one of nine original colonial colleges chartered before the Declaration of Independence was signed. The university boasts the nation's first student union and the first collegiate business school, Wharton. The Greek Revival–style Philadelphia Museum of Art is not far away, its steps mounted in victory in the 1970s by Sylvester Stallone in the movie *Rocky*. And from where I stood next to Mr. Franklin, I could just make out Center City's skyline and the statue of William Penn atop city hall, once the tallest building in the city, now dwarfed by the high skyline that formed in the years since I left home.

Penn had become my most regular client in my higher education consulting practice, an irony seldom lost on me when I visit campus. As a senior at Marple Newtown High School in the Philly suburbs, I never would have been accepted at Penn as a freshman, or any Ivy League for that matter. I began my college career instead at Drexel University, a good regional school adjacent to Penn geographically and renowned for its cooperative education program and easier entrance for capable suburban kids like me whose admission qualifiers were well shy of the Ivy threshold at the time.

For me, the leafy Penn campus represents more than a nostalgic return to my hometown. It represents the complex web of human relationships I find on any college campus I have served or consulted for. "Welcome to the Penn Bubble," a member of the residential life staff offered during one of my early consulting engagements. I learned then something that has been underscored in the years since. The University of Pennsylvania is an incredible, well-resourced institution full of ambition and innovation. In some ways, it is unique. In others, it feels all so familiar as I coach academic and administrative staff. At Penn and through the higher education industry, its people are without question its greatest asset and its largest budget expense. Also, its people provide the greatest coaching challenge for those I support.

STAY IN YOUR ENERGY

I encourage my clients to look at all the people within their sphere—their bosses, their colleagues, and their direct reports—through the lens of newness. Think about how you felt about people when you were new in your current role, basking in the sun of your administrative honeymoon. People may have said things to you along the lines of "Thank God you are here. Your predecessor was a disaster." This happens a lot, and it can feel like an endorsement for you to put your unique stamp on your role, until you are on the other side of it and someone is placing their unique stamp on what you are most proud of upon your departure.

When we are new in our roles, we experience the full spectrum of sensations, from a high of euphoric "what could be" to a low of festering problems that were not fully addressed before we arrived (e.g., "Let's let the new person tackle that"). And it is this kind of fresh energy, the energy of first impressions and of innocent questions, that we need to hold onto well beyond our listening tours.

Our current role and the current mix of people with whom we engage are not eternal. We will one day move on. So will they, including the extraordinary tone setters we admire and the colleagues who drive us nuts. It is all impermanent.

Unless we are starting an office from scratch, there existed an organizational reality BU, *Before Us*, that we can't swiftly categorize into good or hot mess. There are likely traditions, behaviors, and values that have merit and deserve to be honored. Others will naturally shift as we develop our confident voice. Also, one day the job will no longer be ours, and there will be a new reality, AWAG, *After We Are Gone*. Our contract period will end. We will move to our next professional chapter or retirement. Or maybe the campus needs will change, and all involved will naturally arrive at the unspoken but clearly understood "It's time." A farewell gathering will be held, gifts and kind words exchanged, and both we and the institution will move on. We will be remembered as we have remembered those who came before us. But for now, here we are today, living right smack in the middle, between BU and AWAG.

BRING PEOPLE ALONG

Some campus roles lend themselves to relationships more than others. During a Fulbright administrators' program in Germany and Poland I was part of some years ago, I was surrounded by career services practitioners who were very much like me. During the three-week trip, we developed reputations for fully engaging our European hosts as we visited universities and vocational institutes. We were known to establish rapport with our hosts, ask plenty of questions, eagerly exchange our business cards, and identify programmatic spots of common ground. A higher education colleague sitting next to me on the bus at the end of a long travel day said, "You career services people are so good at networking. It's like you are in sales or something." I took my colleague's remark as a compliment as the bus pulled up to our hotel in Munich that evening. Certain higher education professions, including career services, community relations, alumni engagement, advancement, and student services lend themselves to bridge-building across many stakeholder groups. And people in these disciplines are often the tone setters to watch as they dance within their organizational networks.

But what may come easy for those of us with extraverted personalities may take more effort for those colleagues for whom relationships seem less important. I am currently working with a client who has a keen scientific mind and is working as part of a team in a donor-funded university start-up dedicated to health disparities among LGBTQ+ people. She is passionate, sharp, and clear-eyed about her work goals and objectives. Her challenge is that while the work calls for a team approach to problem-solving, she is the ultimate solo operator. This is stressing her, and her aloof behaviors are impacting the esprit de corps of her project team.

I was naive about this early in my campus career. I remember developing my first Career Discovery Week for students, a series of events including lectures, panel discussions, a keynote, and a small information fair. I was tasked with raising money to support the week and with collaborating with others in the office to pull it off. I had no direct reports at the time except for a few library assistants. I cherished the sense of control, and I was determined to do it all on my own, which I did. By the end of an exhausting week of programs, I didn't feel any glory really. None of my colleagues had any skin in the game because I didn't bother to include them. My boss wrote me a handwritten note at the end of the Career Discovery Week, praising my vision and organization and cautioning me to include more people in the planning and execution of my future programs. For me, my first Career Discovery Week was an empty victory. Lesson learned.

Tone setters, even if introverted, become comfortable connecting easily with a wide range of stakeholders—their colleagues, their bosses, their student assistants, their teams, and countless other stakeholders with whom they can inform, persuade, and partner. They understand that all these people-oriented people are part of a vast, ever-changing, living and breathing, sometimes fragile ecosystem. "Andy, you need to go where the energy is," one of my wise bosses offered when I was absorbed by a gnarly HR issue. Tone setters seek out the energy in others and plug into it.

Of all the clients I have supported, a common coaching emphasis tends to center not just on other people but on how to supervise them, motivate them, get along with them, collaborate with them, and overcome conflict with and among them. Our sessions often center around "the other" in my clients' professional lives, or as we call it in the coaching world, the ghost in the room. The ghost is the demanding boss, the unreasonable faculty member, the needy direct report, or the competitive colleague. None of these individuals are in the coaching session with us. Yet, if I let them, they can consume so much of our strategic discussion.

Why can't we simply fix these others? Tone setters know that this is an impossibility. They also know that we can actually learn from them and strengthen our own tone. As Stephen Nachmanovitch writes in *The Art of Is: Improvising as a Way of Life,* "We know ourselves through each other."

PEOPLE SURPRISE US

While doing my early listening tour in one of my roles, our university's director of student health and one of my colleagues on the vice chancellor's leadership team warned me that one day I would be sued as an administrator. He deadpanned that this was merely a rite of passage, kind of a sick administrative hazing ritual. "Brace yourself," he said without even a modest grin on his face. I laughed it off, thinking, *You don't know me. I would never let that happen.* My colleague was serious.

Two years later, I was whistle-blown by an unnamed university employee. No, it wasn't exactly a lawsuit, but it did lead to a six-month investigation of my utilization of state funds. I, along with my business manager, were subpoenaed to release my Outlook calendar for the past two years, identifying every meal I had at the faculty club, with whom, and how payment was made, including screen shots of every check I wrote for personal meals. As a faculty club member, I had an account where I paid out of pocket for personal lunches and casual lunch dates with campus colleagues, and I was permitted to use my office funds for business-related meals, such as with key alumni or employers. My vice chancellor was brought into the mix, and after an incredibly humiliating "Andy, I need you to be more careful" conversation, the case was closed and I was deemed innocent. But for me, the damage was done.

We learn that wherever we go, we will come up against people, power, and politics. We need to remember that we, too, are part of the people, power, and politics. I learned from this difficult experience that the issue was not as clean as right and wrong. It was about optics, the perceptions that others may have of our work, our privilege, and our priorities.

As difficult as it was to be whistle-blown, it was heartwarming to receive gestures of support after my mother died early on in my career. In addition to cards of condolence, my campus colleagues prepared for me enough food to last for a week as I began to grieve her loss. And they all chipped in to purchase a small maple tree in her honor, which I planted in my front yard. It's been decades since I sold that home, and in a recent visit I drove by that house. My mother's maple, once no more than three feet in height, now towered over the rooftop, providing dappled shade on a sunny afternoon.

People surprise us, in bad ways and especially in good. Our tone setters take it all in with equanimity, rejoicing in the moments of kindness and grieving in those times of mistreatment before moving on.

TONE SETTER MINDSETS

Working with people potentially presents the biggest stretch for tone setters. They discover that their innovation and thought leadership, all the great ideas they have that generate impact—none of them happen, at least not in a significant way, without the buy-in, collaboration, and ultimate cooperation of people. Even for those whose work may appear quite independent, tone setters know that their professional success and their professional fulfillment are interconnected with their relationships.

MINDSET #26
Establish a relationships file.
There is no way most of us can remember the details of all the people we meet on campus. You might consider developing an alphabetical file of campus relationships that call for special attention, especially with colleagues outside your chain of command. Your file might include notes

from interactions you have had, observations about priorities, even birthdays and the names of family members and pets if they come up. At first glance, this strategy may feel shallow and disingenuous. With that I firmly disagree. As a client who works in a university's research lab said to me recently, "I am trying to become less of a robot." For him that means doing more than his job. It means moving beyond tasks and getting curious about people's lives. I've been there, having received thematic feedback early in my career that I was admired for my productivity but cautioned about my tendency to be a "flyby" colleague, always on the go but rarely pausing long enough to get to know others. A relationships file enabled me to pay more attention to the wholeness of those with whom I served.

MINDSET #27

Welcome newcomers with a lagniappe.

Lagniappe, pronounced lan-'yap, is one of my favorite words. It's a Louisiana Cajun term loosely defined as an extra and unexpected benefit. Order a dozen bagels, and there may be a thirteenth in your box. Book a standard king room at the conference hotel, and receive a complimentary upgrade to a suite. Ask a friend to house-sit while you are away, and come home to a beautiful flower bouquet on your kitchen counter. These are beautiful surprises that land well above our expectations. Be the colleague who takes new hires to lunch, invites someone you serve with on a committee but don't know well to coffee, offers to take a campus stroll with an administrator just back from leave, or gives a visitor from another university a tour of your space. Such thoughtfulness gives you the opportunity to surprise someone with a small gift that can make their day.

MINDSET #28

Listen with openness.

Tone setters know how to listen to those with whom they engage, to really listen. As Steven Covey once said, "Our biggest communication problem is that we do not listen to understand. We listen to reply." In executive coaching terms, that's called Level 1 listening. There is nothing wrong with keeping the conversation going and offering a sense of common ground. But Level 1 listening can quickly hijack the conversation, making it about the listener instead of the one who merely wants to be heard. It becomes a competition of who is the most interesting when it should be about the listener being incredibly interested. Level 2 listening is about creating space for someone to share without judgment. You do not need to nod or say "I get that." You don't need to fix anything or spout words of wisdom. You simply need to be present and say things like "What else?" or "That sounds hard" or "You seem excited about this." Listening with the openness of Level 2 allows people to open up. It's incredibly liberating for them and equally informative for you.

MINDSET #29

Optimize complementary relationships.

There are so many lateral relationships on our campuses that, if tended to, can bolster our success if skillfully managed. If you are responsible for the recruitment and performance of staff, your relationship with Human Resources is vitally important. You can't execute any of the talent work without them. If you manage resources, divisional finance officials can be tremendous allies. If you plan big events, the campus facilities and events staff can be your best friend. The same is true for your parking and transportation staff, your training and development group, and many others across your campus with whom you engage on a regular basis. Just as you seek to work with nice people, so do they.

MINDSET #30

Balance vulnerability with low-drama steadiness.

We may have a sense that we need to demonstrate that we are capable of doing everyone else's jobs. We can't. Nor do we need to translate our expanded responsibilities into unnecessary control. We can let our hair down, and we will surprise ourselves when we realize that people appreciate knowing us as complex humans, not just as administrators. I was once told by a staff member on a campus team that I led that she appreciated my vulnerability. At first, I questioned her remark. Was that a good thing, I wondered? I came to realize that she was commenting on how she felt that she could know me, understand my values, see in my office some things that I treasure, and hear in my meeting facilitation how multidimensional I was and how I could own my flaws. She gave me permission to be something other than perfect.

Mindset #31

Develop your network of Anam Caras.

Popularized by Irish author John O'Donohue, our *Anam Caras* are our "soul friends." There are times we need such friends to cheer us on, and there are times we need them to call us on our delusions. Tone setters cultivate an eclectic group of besties who ably pivot between both roles. These are the people we call when we want to float a brilliant idea, and these are our coffee dates and Zoom chats when we are struggling with a prickly political crisis. Our *Anam Caras* have our backs, and they get us out of our heads. Their role is not merely to puff up our vanity (though every now and again we need that kind of soothing balm!). Include among your *Anam Caras* people you deem to be tone setters, living their lives on campus in a way that you notice, maybe even admire. And as a plug for coaching, consider a trained and qualified coach or other care provider to add to your network. I have one client who counts me as a coach among what she calls her care team—which includes her therapist, her spiritual director, and her yoga instructor!

Mindset #32

Keep people who have supported you in the loop.

Your relationship file should include the *Anam Caras* and tone setters who have positively influenced your choices. All of us appreciate hearing of the success of those we have supervised, mentored, and worked alongside. Make the effort to go beyond blanket LinkedIn life updates (although those are valuable) and send personalized cards, emails, or texts to thank them for the tone setting influence they provided you and their role in your trajectory. This is such an easy thing to do, and it is so overlooked by most people. Yet it can be a tremendous day-maker for those whose lives have touched our own.

MINDSET #33

Bring in the outliers.

The reason we tell our student leaders to bring their friends to events is because we know they are opinion leaders with their peers. We call it friend dragging. These students have the capacity to engage the disenfranchised. They also help us ensure reasonable head counts at our events. The same holds true for us when we know of colleagues who are operating on the fringe of campus and have the capacity to become bigger contributors ... if only someone would invite them. Be that tone setter that finds ways to bring in these people. Invite them to attend an event you are coordinating or serve on a committee you are chairing or play a role on a task force that needs the perspective of someone outside the inner circle. When we rise to a place on campus where we have access or privilege, we then have an opportunity to "drag along" colleagues with potential, to expose them to people or opportunities they would not have opportunity to pursue without our invitation.

POWERFUL QUESTION

What are three actions you might take—to improve a relationship with a direct report, to establish a new relationship with a colleague, and to enhance your relationship with your supervisor?

CHAPTER 6

ENVIRONMENT

TAP THE CAMPUS ENERGY

The responsibility of an architect is to create a sense of order, a sense of place, a sense of relationship.

—RICHARD MEIER

OUR MODERN CAMPUSES are like mini cities. We have clusters of green spaces and quads, bustling student centers with the smell of pizza wafting from woodfire ovens, flyer-plastered kiosks and bulletin boards promoting poetry slams and ride shares for the upcoming vacation break, sprawling athletic fields with the coaching sounds of soccer drills, and that one hideously ugly building on all of our campuses—you know the one on yours. Today's campuses not only nurture the idea of collective energy, they enshrine it.

Think about your favorite campus haunts—like that cozy lounge in the library, or the see-and-be-seen faculty club where administrative power deals are struck, or the java spot where you hold casual meetings and perk up your day, or the campus loop where you power walk to clear your head after a hard-fought budget discussion. All these special places help inform our purpose and fuel our energy—that is, if we are paying attention.

Whether your campus is a traditional collection of structures and quads or several floors in an urban office building, there is a good chance that your school's planners have been especially adept at creating environments to accomplish a number of integrated goals: to inspire learning, to promote creativity, and to facilitate human connection.

And this offers us a kind of motivational superpower against which no other industry can compete. Your campus provides a source of energy you can tap.

THE CLAREMONT COLLEGES

You wouldn't know it when battling truck traffic to exit the snarled I-10 in LA's hazy Inland Empire that less than a mile from the freeway and just off Indian Hill Boulevard sits the storybook community of Claremont, California, an idyllic, walkable village of quaint gift shops, locally owned restaurants, and even a nostalgic old-school drug store. Everything in Claremont is adorable. Local officials proclaim it to be a city of "leaves and PhDs." Its streets are shaded under the canopies of American elms, redwoods, and maples. Claremont is also home to a collection of five prestigious undergraduate liberal arts colleges and two graduate schools, employing 3,600 faculty and staff and educating 9,000 students. I had taken a job at one of them, Claremont McKenna College, working remotely from my Northern California home four hundred miles up the coast and directing the college's distinctive Silicon Valley Program, a study-away semester for students wishing to gain work experience and connections in high-tech start-ups.

I needed to be in Claremont on a monthly basis for student coaching and administrative meetings. I would usually be in town for two or three nights, staying at the hip Casa 425 Hotel in Claremont Village. I would awaken each morning before the sun rose, toss on my runners, shorts, and a T-shirt, and get my steps in by power walking through the five distinct undergraduate Claremont Colleges. The Five Cs, as they are called, stand among this country's "Potted Ivies" given their Ivy League selectivity, their top-of-market price tags, their enviable faculty-to-student ratios, and their combined 540 acres of meticulously landscaped grounds.

I would often begin my brisk walk by heading across the massive grass quad of Pomona College, founded in 1887 and the oldest in the consortium. Within ten minutes and a faster heart rate, Pomona's neoclassical architecture gave way to more brutalist buildings as I stepped onto the main walkway of the premiere science and engineering campus of Harvey Mudd College, founded in 1955. Mudders, as the college's students are called, would still be asleep in their blocky dormitories as I passed by, stepping across a street and entering through a gate onto the walled grounds of Scripps College, founded in 1926 as Claremont's all-women's school with its white-washed stucco walls and tile roofs in the Spanish colonial style. A few minutes later, I was climbing up a slight slope to a vastly different campus, Pitzer College, founded in 1963 with its open spaces covered with native and drought-resistant landscaping. I reached my next stop as the sun rose, and I stepped onto the adjacent Claremont McKenna College campus, founded in 1946 and set up like a barbell with large distinctive structures at either end and classroom buildings and residence halls lining the path in between, reminiscent of California's midcentury modernist movement. Later that day, CMC's elegant supper club, the Athenaeum, would be filled with well-dressed students, faculty, and a dynamic guest speaker.

My sneakers touched all five campuses in just under ninety minutes, with more than seven thousand steps on my iPhone tracker to show for myself. And more importantly, each of these campuses offered endless possibilities for students, faculty, and administrative staff to reflect, create, connect, and reboot.

LEVERAGING YOUR CAMPUS ENVIRONMENT

As intoxicating as I found the Five Cs to be, to really understand the thought that goes into the construction of a college campus, we need look no further than one of our founding fathers and the place where my higher education career began. The opening of the University of Virginia in 1819 was perhaps our richest example of an intricately developed campus master plan. Thomas Jefferson called it an Academical Village, an identifier still used today. Jefferson, who considered himself an architect, rendered intricate blueprints of the campus infused with elements of Palladian and neoclassical design. The campus, or rather the university's Central Grounds, is now a UNESCO World Heritage site. So even our founding university leaders recognized the importance of not only the *why* and *how* of learning but the *where*.

My early work at Virginia and my back-and-forth to the Claremont Colleges underscores the importance of our geography as administrators. Space matters. Jefferson realized that. Bricks, mortar, hardscape, and landscape affect our experience as campus tone setters. Combined as our built environment, these physical aspects of our day-to-day can either boost or drain our wells of energy. I learned in my early department store retail career how to creatively merchandise a floor to inspire shoppers and generate sales. Our campus architects and planners are equally adept at curating spaces—to foster learning, community, and pride of place.

Just as I would comparison-shop other department stores, walking the sales floors of our rivals to observe their point-of-sale strategies, I've comparison-shopped countless campuses to understand what makes each of them so compelling. I am known to wander a campus on a holiday weekend, nose to the glass of locked buildings so that I can see inside. I remember one road trip early in my higher education career where I dropped in on several campuses as I drove down the Pacific Coast Highway from the Bay Area to Los Angeles. I wandered the walkways of fog-enshrouded San Francisco State University, located ironically in the city's Sunset district. I drove around Stanford University, taking pictures of the 160 Canary Island palms lining its impressive entrance to a grand oval and a campus loop, meandering like a ribbon that wraps around the eight-thousand-acre campus. I marveled at the athletics complex at Cal Poly San Luis Obispo. I dodged hurried cyclists as I crossed bike-only lanes on UC Santa Barbara's sprawling oceanfront campus. I stood high on the hill at Pepperdine University, taking in the breathtaking view California's Pacific Coast Highway and Malibu's oceanfront beach homes. And I snacked on a sandwich in the center of UC Irvine's "ring," a lush central park around which the manicured Orange County campus is wrapped.

I learned then that awe is all around us on our campuses and that sometimes we need to get out of our predictable routines and do some wandering in order to experience it. Whether you achieve your life's work at an urban, suburban, or rural college or university, you have what those of our friends in corporate don't have. University of California, Berkeley psychologist Dacher Keltner focuses his research and his Greater Good Science Center on our experience of awe. In his book *Awe: The New Science of Everyday Wonder and How it Can Transform Your Life*, he describes awe as "the feeling of being in the presence of something vast that transcends your understanding of the world." Dr. Keltner may as well be describing a university campus.

I am often surprised that my coaching clients don't pursue awe by leveraging the physical aspects on their campuses. I recently suggested to a client from SUNY's Binghamton University that following our Zoom coaching session, he carve out thirty minutes to take a walk and clear his head. He thought it seemed like a good idea, and he mentioned that the entire campus is contained within a massive nature preserve home to deer, beaver, and over two hundred species of birds. He confessed that even though the preserve sits yards from his office, he had never taken advantage of its meticulously maintained walking trails.

I asked another client at UCLA if she ever found reason to wander through her campus museum to get her creative juices flowing. "Which one?" she asked, informing me that her hilly Westwood campus curates not one but two museums. The Fowler Museum showcases past and present works from Asia, Africa, the Pacific, and the Americas, while the Hammer Museum features overlooked and contemporary artists. She had been to neither.

A third engagement found me on a colorful autumn day at Siena College, a shaded liberal arts gem near Albany, New York. I was working with a team of five in a residence hall conference room on the development of vision, mission, and values for their donor-named student center. After a productive morning of flip-charting aspects of their organizational identity and a tasty chicken fajita lunch, courtesy of their campus catering services, I asked if they would be willing to take an "awe walk" with me. They agreed and off we went on an autumn walking tour, the air crisp and the canopy of trees a wash of orange, red, and gold.

Another client I was visiting at the University of Washington was trying to manifest inspiration during a slow-going strategic planning process. I asked him if there was a special place, outside his office, where he could get into flow as he sketched out his plan. He thought for a moment. Then he abruptly stood up and said, "Come with me." We donned our umbrellas and walked briskly around UW's Drumheller Fountain, heading for the university's most famous building, Suzzallo Library, described as the soul of the Seattle campus. Dating back to the 1920s, Suzzallo's collegiate Gothic style stood proud against the gray skyline. Once inside, we climbed the vast building's grand staircase to a breathtaking 250-foot gilded reading room, rising to a vaulted ceiling sixty-five feet in height. The grand space was illuminated by leaded glass windows incorporating Renaissance medallions. What a brilliant setting to write a strategic plan!

All my clients are looking for ways to discover and inspire their tone. Recently, a longtime client at Australia's University of Sydney invited me into his office with an apology: "Oh, Andy, you would be mortified. I have been in my new office for six months and haven't hung a single picture. It's like no one works here." He chuckled as he took in the sour expression on my face.

It is natural that we come to take our surroundings for granted, living our professional lives in a sliver from parking garage to office, where we do our most important work, or so we think. I invite you to inspire your space and broaden your footprint, allowing the unique nature of your campus spaces to fuel your energy. When was the last time you stepped away from your office and took a walk across campus? Or strolled through your student union? Or sat for meditation or prayer in your campus chapel? Or grabbed a bagel in your dining hall and enjoyed it as you sat next to a group of students? How about a wander through one of your academic buildings, perusing the clutter of flyers on department bulletin boards or the donor plaques in lobbies?

What Makes an Inspiring Space?

I was on a design consulting project for Stony Brook University some years ago, and as part of the project I had the opportunity to interview one of North America's early feng shui masters. Our conversation was one of the highlights of the project as I learned a number of key themes that are central to the practice of feng shui, themes that can be applied to our individual and collective campus environments.

I invite you to pause this chapter until you are sitting at your desk in your office. Then see if you can answer the following nine questions:

1. Does your office feel spacious? Whether large or small, can you create an atmosphere of openness, transparency, and flow? Are there unnecessary boxes around? Or piles on the floor? Or extra file cabinets or furnishings that need to find another home?

2. Is your office well illuminated? Do you benefit from lighting sources from above (ceiling lights), on your work surface (desk and task lighting), and on the floor or on a table (accessory lighting)?

3. Is your space vibrant? What color choices do you have for your walls or for wall art?

4. Is your office environmentally friendly? If you are fortunate to have a window, is it clean? Do you have flourishing live plants? Is your space well ventilated, via a fan, an open window, or properly functioning air-conditioning? How does your office smell?

5. Is your space activated 24-7? When you are not there, what do people see when they walk by your door?

6. Is your office inviting? Is it memorable to visitors? Is there something about it that sparks inspiration in you and a positive feeling in others?

7. Is your space discrete? Do you have appropriate cabinets or closet storage to stow away items that you only need on an infrequent basis?

8. Does your space showcase pride? Or, as I often ask, is your space HGTV-ready? Or do you have to apologize to colleagues and guests for your poor office standards?

9. Is your space structured for multiple work approaches? Do you have a standing desk? Can you switch your computer or laptop to create different backgrounds for Zoom calls?

TONE SETTER MINDSETS

Think about it. All our big tech, from Microsoft to Apple and Google, have modeled their environments on higher education's college campuses. Our industry was there first. You have the most extraordinary workplace to explore and appreciate. The architecture and footprint of your campus, along with the students, staff, and faculty who inhabit it—this is an extraordinary combination. Dare I say your college campus is a sacred place, and it is meant to be fully experienced, even by you—*especially* by you. Soak it in.

MINDSET #34

Take an awe walk.

Your school tells a story—every pathway, every quad, every laboratory, every space. I remember late-night walks as an undergraduate at Virginia Tech after parties. I would cross the university's expansive drill field between the dorms and Burruss Hall and think to myself, *This campus is incredibly beautiful!* as I stumbled back to my apartment. It is a shame how easily that sense of awe can be lost when the once-magical campus becomes our day job. So I recommend regular walks of intentionality to more fully appreciate the built environment that surrounds you. Stop by the art gallery for its new exhibit. Stroll by the sand volleyball courts by the residence halls and watch a game. Check out the new logo merch in the bookstore. Or, and this is a favorite, take a flyer walk, glimpsing the clutter of announcements on bulletin boards and kiosks throughout campus trumpeting student bake sales, theater productions, poetry slams, rooms for rent, and coding marathons. You will be surprised how much information is right there before you as you absorb all that breathes life into your community.

MINDSET #35

Hold important gatherings in your most inspiring spaces.

There are surely plenty of windowless and poorly ventilated conference rooms on your campus, aren't there? Avoid them if you can, and be sure that staff gatherings within your responsibility—especially full-day meetings, retreats, and presentations where the stakes are high—are held in the most inspired campus venue you can arrange. Scheduling lovely venues has become more and more difficult on our venue-constrained campuses, but you owe it to yourself, and those whom you gather, to create inspiration with your meeting locations. One of my clients found a jaw-dropping retreat venue on the top floor of a residence hall with 360-degree view of the campus below. Another struck a deal with the curator at the university archaeological museum and staged an important strategic gathering in one of its ancient galleries. A third pulled some strings to host an important meeting at an affiliated oceanography institute with an unobstructed view of the ocean. Start a list of possible venues you might utilize when the agenda is important and the need for good will and energy is strong.

MINDSET #36

Discover your colleagues' inspired campus locations.

The notion of management by wandering is by no means an original idea, but it has become a lost art for busy administrators. Try conducting some meetings with direct reports and colleagues by asking them to select a campus destination that is significant for them and walk there together, hands free of phones and folders. Challenge yourself to cover the agenda while experiencing the campus through your colleague's eyes. This immediately transforms just another meeting into a healthy and meaningful conversation infused by the energy of the campus. You learn something new, and your colleague is in the driver's seat.

MINDSET #37

Shake up your "to and from" routines.

Mindfulness guru Jon Kabat-Zinn asks "The little things? The little moments? They aren't little." Such a simple yet wise statement. Often when I am working with a senior administrator who is feeling stuck on the job, we discuss the limiting nature of certain routines, and I challenge the client to get back to a place of creative expression by shaking things up. For example, you might take a more scenic route to campus or change your mode of transportation, even if it adds ten minutes to the commute. Once on campus, maybe approach the office from a different direction. Don't use the back door to your office as you often do. Enter through the main door as if you were a student or client. Get to meetings across campus with time to spare to increase the potential of informal chat before the printed agenda is passed.

MINDSET #38

Curate your personal space.

Nine times out of ten, when I work with an administrator experiencing overwhelm, we can look at their office and see a lack of inspiration. Either the space looks like they could pack up and vanish within five minutes, or it's dusty, grimy, and cluttered. What they don't recognize is that their space does matter, a lot. Even tidying expert Marie Kondo has taken her clean-it-up evangelism to the workplace in her book *Joy at Work* with coauthor Scott Sonenshein. You don't have to become an interior designer if that's not your thing, but you could add some lamps, art, and other personal effects to show that you care. It will make the space work better for you and for those who visit you.

MINDSET #39

Show that you are open for business.

Along with our newfound flexibility following the COVID-19 pandemic, we find that our hybrid schedules have created an unintended ghost-town environment in many offices and centers on our campuses. It is rare when an office is fully staffed anymore. These dark hallways and locked doors are not what campus designers had in mind when they envisioned vibrant environments for teaching and learning. To what-ever extent is possible, demonstrate that your area is open to campus foot traffic. Turn the lights on (if environmentally appropriate). Hire a responsible student worker to serve as concierge to greet people. Open some doors that won't set off alarms.

MINDSET #40

Add ritual to your space.

If you work in a suite of offices that has been renovated, have an open house to welcome colleagues into your refreshed space. If you work in a new space, consider a dedication, christening, or ribbon cutting. The point is to allow your cube, office, suite, or building to become a wel-coming space for community. Invite people in! This demonstrates your pride for your environment and gratitude for working on a campus that creates meaningful spaces to work, learn, and connect.

POWERFUL QUESTION

What does a welcoming campus environment look like, and how might you establish one?

PART THREE

SOFTENING YOUR EDGES

D URING A RECENT walkabout at the University of Hawaii at Manoa, I found myself gazing intently at a flyer on a bulletin board entitled *Mindfulness: Weekly Sessions for the Spring Semester*. This student-centered program promised to enhance focus and attention, reduce stress, decrease reactivity, and increase resilience.

"Is this popular?" I asked my colleague, a longtime California administrator who traded in campus life on the mainland for the aloha spirit and island trade winds of Oahu.

"Absolutely! This is a priority of my dean," she said. "The students all get subscriptions to Headspace!" she added, referencing one of the top meditation apps many of us download on our phones.

If students can benefit from such edge softeners, then so can we who are paid to guide, challenge, and inspire them. The founder of the San Francisco Zen Center, Shunryu Suzuki, was often quoted as saying, "You are perfect, just as you are … and you can use a little improvement." It is the text after the ellipses that will drive our discussion in this next section. Since we are working in academies of learning, our higher education careers provide tremendous opportunity for us to continue to develop our learning muscles and to soften the jagged edges that sabotage the tone we wish to set.

In the chapters ahead, let's take an honest look at some imperfections—the imperfection of our real and imagined behavioral limitations, the discomfort we feel when we stagnate and lose our drive for the work, and our response to the growing organizational disruptions on our campuses.

CHAPTER 7

LIMITATIONS
Pursue Your Growth

There is a crack in everything. That's how the light gets in.
—Leonard Cohen

A s you go about your daily campus b usiness, you wouldn't know that limitations even exist. If your school is anything like the ones I've served, its entrance is bedazzled with banners broadcasting superlatives like We're the best and the brightest! or Divisional Champions! or You define the future! Affirming messages like these can bolster us as we do our administrative work. We may find ourselves getting wrapped up in all the hype as we glance at all those certificates that line our offices. We've earned those accolades. Or have we?

The word "failure" is never uttered in our campus lexicon. Our institutional messaging, in its entirety, is about possibility, potential, and ultimate success. So goes our ratings-driven higher education world. We speak only the language of good to better, never mediocre to subpar. For those of us operating from the middle of our schools' administrations, we need to expand our self-awareness beyond boosterish "You're number one!" slogans. We need to hold up a mirror to our limitations so that we can do the important work of owning them and editing them.

It may seem counterintuitive, but there is a beauty in owning our flaws, symbolized by the ancient artform of *kintsugi*. It is a Japanese technique of mending in which broken or damaged pottery is reassembled with a gold-powdered lacquer. The resulting pieces, held together with meandering gold veins all around, appear intentional in their artistry. They are each unique, and their imperfections only enhance their value and their authenticity. This tradition of *kintsugi* can teach us about how to handle the "broken" bits of ourselves that feed into our administrative roles.

I knew nothing about *kintsugi*. Nor did I have much exposure to failure when was invited to innovate at a university on the other side of the globe.

UNIVERSITY OF MELBOURNE

The city tram rattled its way down Swanston Street in Melbourne, Australia. I stepped off at Flinders Street station, the city's frenetic transportation hub and gathering place, just in time for the start of a weekly mindfulness ritual. As I found my seat on a folding chair in the chaotic plaza, a robed monk stepped gingerly onto the stage, positioning himself in a more comfortable armchair as he turned on his microphone. A moment later, the monk tapped a small gong as he asked, "Can we invite the bell?" As if on cue, his assembled audience of one hundred closed its eyes, bowed its heads, and sat in silence for guided meditation.

The buzz of the city was all around—the horns, the tram bells, and the smells of baked bread and falafel wafting from nearby cafés. My head was cluttered. My so-called monkey mind was active, and as I tried to return my focus to the inhale and exhale of my breath as instructed, I imagined what a bizarre spectacle an assembly of meditators must have presented to hurried commuters passing by to catch their trains, grab their to-go lunch meat pies, or walk off the frustration of their morning meetings. We meditators persisted, sitting in silence in the middle of it all, heads bowed, as the city's energy swirled all around us.

I needed something, anything, to get some clarity.

My meditation hour at Flinders Street station was prompted by the ultimate bad morning on the job. I remember staring at my wearied face in the reflection of a glass-topped table. At least the airless conference room where ten of us gathered for a staff meeting boasted an exceptional ninth-floor view from the University of Melbourne's Raymond Priestly Building. The skyline of Melbourne's CBD (central business district) stretched out before us with the Yarra River and Bay of Port Phillip just beyond. Priestly was Melbourne University's secured power tower, as campus staffers called it. The chancellor and all top officials had offices in there, and I, as a project consultant to the university, had access to at least a few of them—that is once I flashed my university identification to the surly building security guard before stepping into the elevator on the ground level.

The staff meeting began. As the agenda was circulated, I put on my glasses as I skimmed our first three discussion items:

1. Utilization of Excel pivot table to track student engagement
2. Global economic crisis: Limits on university discretionary spending
3. Framework for aspirational student life cycle (see attachment)

The agenda was previewed aloud by the director, an administrator from the United Kingdom who demonstrated a real knack for pushing student services innovation at Melbourne. As he read item number three, he circulated an attachment, resulting in some eye rolls among my Australian administrative mates crowded around the table. We all looked down at the diagram placed before us. It looked similar to an ancient coliseum—complete with grand stairs, ornate columns, and a gabled roof. Each element represented a different facet of the student experience, and the word "engagement" appeared no fewer than three times on the image—student engagement, staff engagement, faculty engagement. It resembled a rendering of Caesar's Palace in Las Vegas. One member of the leadership team remarked under his breath, "It looks more like a temple of doom than an aspirational model for student success." I chuckled as I pondered the ultimate fall of the Roman Empire.

As the too-long meeting concluded, the director, who was both my client and my boss, nodded to me and said, "Andy, can you stick around for a few minutes?" "Of course," I responded as the two of us headed down the hall to his office with its massive desk and equally expansive view of Melbourne's northern suburbs. He was my toughest boss to get a read on. Though all who knew him found him quite visionary, his leadership style was absent of affect. It was hard to know where I stood or what he was thinking. Also, he was younger than me, a first in my professional experience. I had always been in roles where I was dutifully pleasing my elders. The words of former Secretary of State Madeleine Albright flashed in my cluttered mind: "The older I am, the younger are my teachers." But what did I have to learn from this administrator?

The director sat at his desk and asked me to take a seat across from him, a shift from our usual chats around his conference table. I knew something was up. "People are wondering where you are," he remarked in his British lilt, usually proper and elegant but more biting in this instance. His eyes didn't rise from his desk as he shared that my performance as a consultant was not what he had hoped. Part of the university's attraction to me was that I was president of an American higher education association and that I would be traveling to the United States on numerous occasions during my contract period. But now I realized what I thought was an advantage was not setting the tone that he and his boss, Melbourne University's provost, were seeking. I was a tone setter all right, but I didn't bother to integrate my go-to tone with the unique needs of the institution.

It took a trusted Australian colleague and friend, Nigel Cossar, to introduce me to a term I'd not heard of. Over a filling Italian lunch on Lygon Street, Melbourne's own Little Italy neighborhood a quick stroll from the university, Nigel cut to it: "Your problem," he explained twirling his pasta, "is that people here see you as a tall poppy."

"A what?" I asked, incredulous.

Nigel went on to describe a cultural phenomenon where organizational systems hold us back because of our notable success, intellect, or privilege. Just as Judy Garland's Dorothy falls asleep in a field of tall poppies in the *Wizard of Oz*, the bright vibrant flowers that surrounded the slumbering heroine remind us of the risk of reaching too close to the sun in our work.

I had to admit, Nigel's description made some sense. I was invited as an American administrator to fix something at the University of Melbourne. I was the pro with the charming accent (to them), trotted around from meeting to meeting and invited to present to numerous groups of very important people. Yet all those positive ego bumps were a kind of balm over my undiagnosed behavioral limitations. This university, as bureaucratic and stuffy as it felt to me, was actually a rather egalitarian kind of place, where at the end of the day all could be resolved over beers at a local pub or taking in a footy game together. All my slick PowerPoint decks, American strategery, and elocutionary gifts, though desirable on the surface and actually necessary to justify my work visa, needed to be activated in a gentler, more humble manner. I needed to pivot from being a spot-lit tall poppy to being a trusted colleague. I needed to become one of my mates.

When I eventually left my consulting role and returned to the United States, my Melbourne staff gave me a framed poster-size photograph of a field of Tasmanian tall poppies. To this day, this glorious image provides a vivid reminder that as tone setters, we walk a balance beam between standing out and fitting in.

BEHAVIORAL LIMITATIONS

Poet, teacher, and storyteller Mark Nepo writes, "Without the ability to face our own demons, we often seek revenge rather than feel what ours is to feel." Although "demons" may feel a tad strong, Nepo makes a great point. To be the tone setters we are meant to be, we need to get over our own hype and get acquainted with our flaws, those repeated behaviors that ultimately do not serve us or others. You can think about your behavioral limitations as inhabiting two quadrants. In one quadrant are those limitations that result from a mismatch between our skills and the realities of our current job on campus. We are not up for the task or we are not learning the work or we are choosing not to fully engage with the work. In the other quadrant, we are limited by mind-based beliefs that are totally manufactured in our heads. They have nothing to do with our skill or capacity. Rather, they are negative scripts we play over and over again. Both ends of the spectrum, and all the shades of negativity in between, stealthily drain our energy. It is the mind-based behavioral limitations that account for 75 percent of our challenge. Maybe they are demons after all.

Behavioral Limitations	
Skill-Based Limitations	**Mind-Based Limitations**
• Insufficient job-specific experience	• Impostor syndrome
• Inflated sense of competence	• Accessorized thinking
• Fixed mindset	• Fighting the opponent
• Mismatch between strengths and role	• Bloated ego
• Promoted beyond ability	• Judging saboteurs

SKILL-BASED LIMITATIONS

On our campuses, potential swirls all around us. We are part of something special, and if we are good-natured, reliable, and politically savvy, we fall into growth opportunities that stretch our expertise. Sometimes that works out. Sometimes it does not. Consider the brilliant professor who becomes department chair, the popular chair who becomes college dean, or the well-connected dean who becomes president. Our industry has made an art form of promoting people based not on job-related expertise but on academic reputation and institutional sentimentality. Have you ever worked for a supervisor who couldn't manage a budget or failed to build a favorable esprit de corps for their direct reports? Did you ever partner with a colleague who could not coordinate a meeting or collaborate on a summary report? I certainly have. At times it felt to me like while I was trying to build a tone-setting administrative career for myself, others were merely dabbling in administration, living out five-year contracts with assurances that they could always return to their tenured research and teaching roles. It was like their administrative role was little more than a favor to the provost, a side gig for which they received a generous stipend and a guarantee for an extensive sabbatical when it was all over. This sounds harsh, and truly I have worked with many excellent academic leaders who are bona fide tone setters in my mind. But their career trajectories are often far different from our own, making it all the more essential for we as administrators to address our skill-based limitations head-on.

Of all the external reviews I have conducted for college and university offices and centers through the years, one question always arises among those who hire me to consult: What are the skills needed to operate successfully in today's campus environment? Increasingly, the modern operational skills most needed stretch well beyond standard position description boilerplate like knowledge of particular software, systems, or professional practices. Today's go-to skills are much, much broader—including skills like savvy, diplomacy, responsiveness, community building, persuasion, and most especially integration. Even on the most siloed of campuses, our biggest opportunity is to set a tone of integration—of academic disciplines, of shared service agreements, and of collaborative programming.

As with me at the University of Melbourne, most of us will face a period in our higher education careers where we lack particular skills needed to not only perform the job but to set the ideal tone to inspire others. This happens all the time in the academy. Here are some examples:

- The gifted student adviser who is promoted to a management role without the skills he needs to manage a team.
- The savvy technologist who is offered a role requiring much more training than she anticipated in order to be competent.

- The vivacious admissions leader who lands a senior enrollment management role where most of his time is spent no longer engaging incoming students and their families but instead pouring over spreadsheets and retention trends.
- The young residence life manager who was in the right place at the right time to fill gaps only to discover she has risen to a managerial and political level well beyond her capacity to deliver.
- The talented and introverted researcher who traded in their lab coat to head up a newly named science center, one that requires constant effusive praising of the lead donor.

None of these examples are surprising, especially in higher education. For those of us approaching our administrative careers from backgrounds that are not scholarly, we are well aware of the administrative glass ceilings we are up against. Few of us will become provosts, presidents, or chancellors. If we are hitting our stride on campus and open to growth opportunities, it's natural that we pursue step-up roles, interim appointments, and assignments that broaden our visibility. Also, with so many vacancies in our administrative ranks, institutional leaders are looking for the path of least resistance to fill key vacancies.

Reputable tone setters who are in house often have the edge, even if in an interim capacity. But that doesn't mean they possess all the necessary skills to effectively perform in their new roles. We owe it to ourselves and our universities to evolve along with the new opportunities we pursue. We must continue to up our skill games to build on our strengths and fill our gaps. We must apply a growth mindset, not a fixed one. With each step we take, there is more to learn, more development to seek out, and more to stretch into as we become a next level tone setter. Skill-based limitations are usually rectified with ease through additional training.

Mind-Based Limitations

While at Melbourne University, I met higher education leaders who were every bit as competent as those I had worked for and alongside in the United States. They, like Americans, tend to think of themselves as highly evolved and up-to-date on the latest research on higher education. But if any of us were to put this book down and attempt to sit quietly in a meditative state as I did during my lunchtime meditation at Flinders Street station, I guarantee we would discover that we all occasionally surrender to limiting behaviors of the mind—responses to our work that serve only to halt our growth, dissolve our impact on campus, and zap us of any fulfillment we might have in our work.

What's going on there? Is it that we become bored? Or maybe an event triggers a competitive streak in us. Perhaps we worry that the other shoe will drop for us professionally. It could be that in the absence of crisp metrics, the qualitative nature of our work causes us to question the concrete impact we are making. Or maybe all of our school's positivity has become strangely toxic for us—creating a mountain of hype impossible for us to climb. When such delusional sentiments arise, they can run roughshod over our values and call into question our purpose. Let's take a look at the most common mind-based limitations.

Impostor syndrome

If you ever feel this way, you are not alone. According to the School of Life, a London-based publisher of personal development texts, impostor syndrome has its roots in a basic feature of human existence, one that we all share. "We feel like impostors not because we are uniquely flawed, but because we fail to imagine how deeply flawed everyone else must necessarily also be beneath their polished surface." In essence, we become so lost in a mindset that we feel is ours and ours alone that we fail to recognize the sheer humanness of feeling like we don't measure up. In fact, our experience of impostor syndrome may not be all that different from anyone else's. I can't tell you the number of times a new coaching client says to me something like, "You know, Andy, I try to put on a good game face and present confidence to my administration, but as I step up to deliver an important presentation to my alumni board or contribute meaningfully in a senior staff meeting, I'm thinking to myself, 'If they only knew how insecure I am.'"

Mindfulness guru Tara Brach offers another way to look at the impostor. As one of a number of highly regarded Buddhist luminaries, Brach underscores what she calls our trance of unworthiness. She goes on to describe Buddhism's Four Noble Truths: that suffering exists, that the cause of suffering is delusion, that there is a solution, and that there is a path forward. It is the delusion, the trance, that so often messes with our heads, making us feel not up to the task of the day. More often than not, this lapse in confidence resides only in our heads.

Accessorized thinking

Another belief that can reduce our impact as campus practitioners was identified by Harvard Professor Dr. Susan David, who in her book *Emotional Agility* argues that all our thoughts, good and bad, come accessorized with symbols, colors, and sounds. Some of these accessories are all aspiration and inspiration, while others are dread, paranoia, and other mental minimizers. For example, you can probably relate to the *drumbeat* in the distance of your school's marching band practicing for Saturday's big football game (nostalgia) or the warmth of the *golden afternoon sun* as you headed home at the end of the week when your promotion was announced (contentment). You might also relate to one of your work projects that *crashed and burned* (regret) or the report you delivered that was returned to you by your vice president *marked up in red* (frustration). I hear clients describe programs with questionable outcomes as *clusterfucks* or *shit shows*. Such descriptions are certainly vivid, but if they are overused as qualifiers for our efforts, these images seep into our heads, creating a reality that is never the full truth.

Fighting the opponent

We also relate to the metaphor of competition and an opponent who must be slayed. Popular Wharton professor Dr. Katy Milkman writes in her book *How to Change* that we need to understand our opponent, that internal competitor fighting to hold us back in some way. Our opponent blocks us, trips us, tricks us, and surrenders us to submission if we let it. Father Richard Rohr in his book *Falling Upward: A Spirituality for the Two Halves of Life* describes this phenomenon as our irrational need to "shadowbox" with ourselves. He writes, "I'm sorry to report that shadowboxing continues until the end of life, the only difference being that we're no longer surprised by our surprises or so totally humiliated by our humiliations!" There is nothing wrong with a competitive edge as long as we are not fixated on the win-or-loss outcome.

Bloated ego

Nigel's gentle nudge to soften my approach as a tall poppy was an excellent antidote to a well-intentioned project gone awry, one where I was lost in the delusion of my credibility. I had some work to do, including getting over the ego-infused "if not for me" paradigm.

> *If not for me, these people would still be pulling dog-eared files from cabinets.*
> *If not for me, this place would still be operating in the 1970s.*
> *If not for me, this division would fall apart.*

We have all had these moments, when we feel indispensable and we move into ego mode, circumventing our negative self-talk with unearned self-flattery. I have observed this time and time again in others. Some call it flexing, but I prefer the term peacocking. You've been in meetings where colleagues have flexed their power muscles, publicly proclaiming their ample resources or their sizable staff or their bleeding from the heart about a student issue. What may be intended as commitment and institutional support rarely reads to an audience as good will. Rather, they set a tone of condescension.

According to philosopher and author Ryan Holiday, "Many of us insist that the main impediment to a full, successful life is the outside world." In his book *Ego is the Enemy*, he makes the argument through the stories of famous historical figures that in reality, our most common enemy lies within. Ego stems from fear and from not being seen. On the upside, it differentiates us. It builds our self-esteem. But when not checked or losing ground to others with whom we compete, ego becomes what we must defend. And defend we do.

That's why I am so impressed that the tone setters I know are prone to step away from that, participating in solitary reflective practices where there is no space for a peacock, a tall poppy, a humble bragger, or an impostor by any name. They enjoy hikes with their dog, invest in silent retreats, take to their yoga mats, and get into their minds so they can get out of their heads, like I was attempting to do but with little success at downtown Melbourne's meditation hour. Tone setters step down from the pedestal before others knock them off.

The "if not for me" phenomenon can expand beyond us. Others can plant this in our minds as well. When we are asked to take on a special project or step into an interim role, our boss exclaiming, "I need you for this," it's hard for the ego to remain in check.

A senior leader to whom I reported had the university's chancellor call me on my cell phone. I was caught off guard.

"Andy," the chancellor said, "I am told you are hesitant to take on this role we have created with you in mind. I have a lot of confidence in you, and I really need you for this."

Please understand, I had probably been in the chancellor's office less than a dozen times in my tenure, and though she knew my name, let's be real, she knew very little about me or my capabilities but was advised by others to close the deal to get me into a new role. I was a logical institutional solution to an organizational chess game. I was good enough to help execute the next move on the board.

"Yes, Chancellor Fox," I replied, my hand shaking as I cradled my flip phone. "I appreciate your faith in me, and I am eager to support you and lead this effort."

And that is how I achieved the highest-level role I will ever have in the academy. I remember saying these very words at a party with some top-level campus colleagues: "You know, I was asked by the chancellor to do her a favor." It was heady stuff, for sure. But the message here is that I needed to keep this lofty promotion grounded and do the work—for the sake of the contribution, for the challenge, and for the vast opportunity it offered to address my skill-based limitations. I also needed to extinguish the myth that nothing would happen "if not for me." Life would go on with me or without me in that role.

Judging saboteurs

Clearly there are plenty of labels for the limitations in our heads, and throughout our careers these labels play in our minds in predictable ways. Canadian mindfulness coach Jeff Warren refers to our "destroyer," our "toxic shame," and our "mind trying to eat itself." Gross! When I certified as a positive intelligence coach some years ago, I did so in an attempt to find a new label for the negative energy that would come and go for me and for my clients.

The Positive Intelligence movement, PQ, is based on the best-selling book by Coach Shirzad Chamine by the same name. According the Chamine's research, we can trace our saboteurs back to a time of innocence, when we were kids. Reflect on your childhood self at the age of five, and if you can remember, reflect on what you were like at that age. If we were working together individually, I would ask you to find a photo of yourself at that age. Mine is pinned on my bulletin board in my coaching studio. There I am, wide-eyed in overalls standing in the front yard of my childhood home. I was a good kid, though my three much older brothers remind me I could be a nuisance. I was eager to please my parents, organized in how I kept my bedroom, and resistant to anything resembling conflict (i.e., parents arguing, fights on the playground, teachers yelling).

Like all of us, as I aged and persisted through those awkward teenage years, I began to claim my agency, to find my voice, and those childhood scripts began to subside. But according to Chamine's research, some of these early belief systems that helped us survive physically and emotionally stick with us. In fact, they become full-blown inner personas, called saboteurs, and they greatly limit our potential as adults. They represent a set of automatic habits of our minds, each with its own voice, beliefs, and assumptions that work against our best interest.

Chamine argues that "the first step in weakening our saboteurs is to identify and expose them, as you can't fight an invisible enemy, or one pretending to be your friend." Our primary saboteur is referred to as our judge, and the judge is supported by what are called accomplices. See if any of these ring true for you:

- **Avoider**: focusing on the positive and pleasant in an extreme way. Avoiding difficult and unpleasant tasks and conflicts. *There is absolutely nothing wrong on our campus. It's all good.*
- **Controller**: anxiety-based need to take charge and control situations and people's actions to one's own will combined with high anxiety and impatience when that is not possible. *We would save so much time if my staff would simply do what I say. After all, I am the boss, or should be!*
- **Hyper-achiever**: dependent on constant performance and achievement for self-respect and self-validation. Highly focused on external success, leading to unsustainable workaholic tendencies and loss of touch with deeper emotional and relationship needs. *I am going to be sure that I am the top performer in my department, or why bother? Anything less is utter failure.*
- **Hyper-rational**: intense and exclusive focus on the rational processing of everything, including relationships, often perceived by others as cold, distant, and intellectually arrogant. *Look, people! Regardless of how you feel, the numbers don't lie. Use your heads!*
- **Hyper-vigilant**: continuous intense anxiety about all the dangers and what could go wrong; vigilance that can never rest. *I won't be able to sleep until we get through this big campus event next week. There is a lot at stake.*

- **Pleaser**: indirectly tries to gain acceptance and affection by helping, pleasing, rescuing, or flattering others; loses sight of own needs and becomes resentful as a result. *I gave every member of my staff a bespoke holiday gift. I wish they showed more gratitude.*
- **Restless**: constantly in search of greater excitement in the next activity or constant busyness; rarely at peace or content with the current activity. *I have got a million ideas, but I can't seem to get much accomplished.*
- **Stickler**: perfectionism and a need for order and organization taken too far. *I wish my colleagues had my high standards. This school would run a whole lot better.*
- **Victim**: emotional and temperamental as a way to gain attention and affection; an extreme focus on internal feelings, particularly painful ones. Martyr streak. *I feel like everyone ganged up on me at last week's staff meeting. It's like they are out to get me.*

For you and me in our campus roles, it takes effort to overcome mind-based limiting beliefs. It is important to become intimately familiar with the parts of ourselves that deplete our power. This takes courage and honesty. There is no room for delusion or the hype that surrounds us on campus. Unfortunately, there are plenty of campus professionals (you could probably name some right now) who ignore their need to be accountable for their limitations, instead blaming others for their lost promotion, mediocre performance appraisal, or uncomfortable feelings that more often than not have little to do with their campus experiences. It is not my intent to encourage any of my clients, or you, to tolerate unprofessional treatment or substandard working conditions. Still, if you wish to think like a tone setter, you need to strengthen the muscle of discernment, distinguishing between which of your perceptions are truly a problem and which perceptions are your spin on a reality that is yours to fix, whether skill-based or mind-based. Tone setters know that we can learn to edit our own negative energy, and they know how to manifest personal and professional changes to soften their edges.

If you were to name the negativity that creeps into your mind, as I often ask my clients to do, what would you call it? For me, negativity shows up as the classic Debbie Downer, performed with perfection by Rachel Dratch on an earlier generation of *Saturday Night Live*. She is grating and unpopular, and she can bring any party to a screeching halt with the all-too-familiar sound effect, "Wah, Wah." Come to think of it, it was Debbie who was in my head on that day in Australia.

TONE SETTER MINDSETS

Tone setters meet their limitations, both real and self-diagnosed, head-on. They resist delusions, focusing instead on small pivots and expansive growth. Negativity is part of any career. Tone setters know that. They also know how to find the right skill and job fit and they know how to slay the skill-based and mind-based limitations that may hold them back.

MINDSET #41

Practice self compassion.

We are often our own worst critics. I have seen this in myself and in many I have worked with who aspire to high levels of success. We fail to give ourselves a break, coming down too hard on ourselves during periods of failure. In the last decade, an entire body of literature has formed to address our tendency to beat ourselves up, thanks to the pioneering work of Dr. Kristin Neff, an educational psychology professor at the University of Texas at Austin and author of several books, including *Self Compassion: the Proven Power of Being Kind to Yourself*. On Neff's website, you gain free access to a number of practices, talks, and other resources to be kinder to yourself, especially during those times on campus when you need to show yourself some love.

MINDSET #42

Pursue professional development.

There is no industry more equipped to help us succeed professionally than higher education. Its very reason for being is grounded in human growth. So whatever limitation you may face, whether it is needing to master Excel, bolster your leadership skills, respond productively to interpersonal conflict, or better understand issues of diversity, inclusion, and belonging on your campus—consider pursuing no-cost, low-cost, or deeper investment options. Your eagerness to learn is a key tone setter mindset and one that will pay dividends throughout your career. It places you in active mode, taking charge of your growth in a positive manner.

MINDSET #43

Hire a coach.

We all need a coach from time to time. Through our rhythm of upward mobility, we don't check in with ourselves enough, if at all, to determine whether we are *really* on track—setting our best goals and progressing smoothly through our current role and toward our next professional role. A coach is not a well-intentioned family member, supportive mentor, or caring colleague. Increasingly, senior campus administrators hire a coach to call them out on their limitations and challenge them to up their games. They were once considered a perk for corporate leaders and university presidents, but the *Chronicle of Higher Education* in a recent article on hiring and talent management reported that more campuses are adopting a "culture of coaching" to also assist administrators with strategic thinking and decision-making.

MINDSET #44

Adopt an explorer's mind.

The easiest path is to let your limitations rule the day. After all, we are intimately familiar with them. They represent the path of least resistance and the most well-worn neuropathway. They try to ensure that we expend far too much energy on negatively judging ourselves, judging

others, and judging our situation. But a tone setter processes their negative energy differently, reframing it as an opportunity to investigate
it and replace it with empathy, creativity, and forward momentum.
Picture yourself flying above the limitations that are holding you back,
and use this as an opportunity to gently explore solutions free of anger,
resentment, or any of the negative emotions that so often come easily.

MINDSET #45

Apply a "lean startup" strategy.

An important lesson I learned when supporting liberal arts students
working in internships in Silicon Valley start-ups comes from Eric
Ries's book *The Lean Startup*. It turns out that even driven entrepre-
neurs have a tendency to let their limitations delay the launch of a
new app, tool, or product that could be epic, eventually missing their
opportunity. I see this in my college and university clients as well. Their
self-doubt and their saboteurs hold them back from making the impact
that is in their heart and mind. As Ries explains, any of us can establish
an MVP—that's minimum viable product—and from that move into
a build-measure-learn. "What's the worst that is going to happen?" a
wise tone setter once asked me. Higher education is about experimentation. It's about trying new things and, resources allowing, taking
some calculated risks. Try to innovate in your work before it is perfect.

MINDSET #46

Take an action for which you will receive no recognition.

So many of us who find our way into higher education are pleasers.
Although that sounds positive, when our pleaser is also a saboteur, it
leads us to a relentless drive to do good for the sake of the adoration
it earns us. Consider doing some small acts of kindness, but do them
anonymously. Clean out the shared refrigerator after hours or place
flowers on the reception desk on a Monday morning. Let your colleagues guess who the hidden do-gooder is, and strengthen your skill of
internalizing the reward that comes with doing good.

Powerful Question

What is one limitation you can address
immediately to elevate your tone?

CHAPTER 8

STAGNATION
LISTEN FOR SIGNS OF CHANGE

Where in our upbringing are we explicitly taught to value, to enjoy, even to love the plateau, the long stretch of diligent effort with no seeming progress?
—GEORGE LEONARD

M ANY CONSIDER HIGHER education to be a gentle, compassionate, and forgiving industry for professionals who are busy raising kids, pursuing additional degrees, or caring for family members in need. Even so, a hard-to-measure feeling of stagnation can sneak up on us in our careers. Through all the life juggling and self reminders that "we've got a good thing going, don't mess with it," our nudge of stagnation may be telling us something more profound, and as tone setters we should listen to it with nonjudgmental curiosity.

UNIVERSITY OF ILOILO

It was a chilly morning a few days before Christmas, around 6:30 a.m. I had just fed Dolly her breakfast. Like me, Dolly the cat is an early riser. While she devoured her Fancy Feast pâte, I sipped my coffee next to the fireplace and began my morning news scroll on my iPhone: *New York Times, Inside Higher Education*, LinkedIn, and Facebook. On this particular morning my Facebook Messenger notification was highlighted. I opened a message from a young woman named Mary Rose Altamera.

"Hi Sir Andrew," the message began. "You may not remember me but I'm Rose, an alumna of the University of Iloilo in the Philippines. A few years ago, you were the consultant who visited our school, and I was one of the lucky selected students you chose to conduct a home visit."

I certainly did remember Rose, one of the many students, faculty, and staff I met over the course of multiple visits across three years as a consultant for USAID. I was brought in on a development project to design and enhance career centers on university campuses in the Philippines in order to bolster the employability of their graduates. The University of Iloilo was my designated campus, and Rose was among the many students I met during my visits there.

Founded in 1947, UI held its first classes in huts with bamboo walls and mud floors. These makeshift buildings accommodated ambitious young men and women who had just suffered from World War II. Over seventy years later, UI was educating learners like Rose, young people who come largely from poor families throughout the country's Western Visayas region. As I read Rose's message, I flashed back to the vibrant banners that hung throughout the small walled-in campus. They read I WANT. I CAN. I BELONG!

Rose's Facebook message continued. "At the time you visited me, I had planned not to continue my schooling as my family didn't have enough money. But lucky me, doors of opportunity and privilege began to open after your visit."

I couldn't recall any sense of opportunity or privilege as I boarded a small rickety boat with Rose and several UI officials to make the short fifteen-minute ride over to San Lorenzo Island, where Rose's parents and her eight brothers and sisters lived. Once we docked at a small wharf on the island, we hopped into the back of an open-air jeepney, a prolific vehicle in the Philippines that serves as public transportation in many regions. After thirty minutes of surprisingly smooth roads, our driver pulled off the main thoroughfare, and we bounced around on our benches behind the driver for what felt like a very long final mile before the jeepney came to a stop. There before us was a rather large shack on stilts with tarps patching the roof. The windowless home consisted of one room with a ladder to a second-floor loft space.

The Altamera home was rustic but tidy, and Rose's parents were at an outside dining table, chopping coconuts for juice to serve the small entourage that arrived on their land. Rose's dad didn't look much older than thirty, and with the help of an interpreter, he and I were able to share niceties in English and Tagalog as he welcomed this American into his outdoor home. We sipped our fresh coconut juice before our driver led us back to the jeepney.

An hour later, following another jeepney and boat ride, we were back in Iloilo's chaotic city center where Rose took us to the boarding house where she lived during the week. Although convenient to the university and reported to be a safe, secure place for single girls to live, the substandard building lacked the cleanliness or the warmth of her parent's modest island house. Rose shared a dark two-bedroom with two other students; they apparently took turns, two sleeping in the single beds and the third on the floor. There was no shower, and there was a single doorless toilet that could be seen at the end of a dank hall. We were told it accommodated twenty girls. Outside this slum, laundry hung all around on clotheslines, and a rancid-smelling stream flowed down the neighboring alleyway.

Rose's message continued: "I am so grateful for you. You are an instrument that God used to help me achieve my dream. Now, as I write this, I am a Licensed Professional Teacher, and I am waiting to take my oath. May God continue to bless you, Sir Andrew."

The story of Rose's Facebook message is not about my desire to don my angel wings for you. I suspect Rose's message was tailored to many people whom she wished to thank as she completed her studies. But her note appeared when I was feeling rather stagnant and not sure of where or how to direct my restless energy. Her message provided me a spark on that morning, a glimmer that reminded me that I am never fully aware of the impression I make or the tone I set. The fact that Rose remembered me, sought me out on social media, and took the time to update me on her life journey, well, that was a perfectly timed reminder that what I do has an impact, even years later.

We all get kind messages from people like Rose, don't we? They may be former students, fellow campus staff colleagues, or even direct reports for whom we had provided their biggest professional opportunity. "You're the best boss I ever had," shared one of my direct reports. These serendipitous gifts are unforgettable and sacred, and they need to be gathered, stored, and brought out during the inevitable moments in our higher education careers when we are feeling plateaued.

CAUSES OF STAGNATION

Responding to professional stagnation is about more than saving trinkets and thank-you notes from appreciators, though such things do matter. Even for my college and university clients whose accolades are practically at their fingertips, many will ask themselves, "Why am I losing interest in my work?" Perhaps it is the professional version of the famed seven-year itch. Stagnation may arise when you have outgrown the challenges of your job. You may sense a drop in your once-zealous ambition. Maybe you have had your wings cut and are no longer enjoying the professional freedom you once did. Perhaps you are feeling stuck as others around you move on to new roles. Or maybe you are dealing with unexpected physical challenges. Maybe you feel that the rising commoditization of higher education has left our industry with an outcome you didn't realize you signed on for: inflated grades, lower academic standards, and a drive to pander to external stakeholders—donors, parents, trustees—whose voices have become amplified in our campus design or governance.

There could be countless drivers for our malaise, and it can be helpful to frame the experience as a natural rest stop on our journey as tone setters. Rather than unleashing our saboteurs on all that is wrong with our work world, to understand stagnation we need to hold a mirror to ourselves, examining the root causes of what is changing within us. Fortunately, there is plenty of theory to help guide us. Let's take a look at six phenomena that might explain our stagnation.

Arrival fallacy

One explanation for stagnation is described fully in an *Atlantic* article by author and Harvard professor Arthur Brooks. Brooks argues that it is often the act of reaching the achievement that animates us. So think about when you competed for a campus role on which your sights were set and actually landed it. Or maybe you executed a massive campus event and have just wrapped up its postmortem. Perhaps your staff achieved the elusive targeted freshman yield. Maybe you just concluded the most recent capital campaign. Any of these achievements create obvious psychological bumps. According to the theory of arrival fallacy, once the bliss of success is reached, we return to our equilibrium, our steady state of homeostasis. With that, rather than feeling a warm afterglow, we may feel ragged, disoriented, and in need of a new mountain to climb.

Diderot effect

Another philosophy also plays on the connection between striving and completion. Named for eighteenth-century French philosopher Denis Diderot, the Diderot effect describes a fallacy that stagnation can be overcome by simply accumulating more. The story of Diderot centers on his delight over a beautiful silk dressing gown he acquired. It was so beautiful, in fact, that everything that surrounded it felt drab and cheap by comparison. This led to a frenzy of consumption for Diderot, plunging him into debt and ultimately reducing his happiness. In today's market economy, this phenomenon is commonplace. It is our relentless cognitive dissonance. For example, we renovate our kitchen and decide we need to trade up to higher-grade cabinets, a new floor, and the wine refrigerator that was not part of the original estimate. The same can be applied to our campus experience. With the fanfare of our recent promotion, our new office space, or the rock-star direct reports we recruited all behind us, we wonder why our jubilation was short-lived and look for ways to accumulate more—a bigger portfolio, more budget responsibility, easier access to higher level meetings, or a title bump to match our self-perception of our contributions. We respond to our stagnation by trying to add more trinkets of success, never pausing to understand what we already possess.

U-shaped happiness curve

Diderot's plight aligns with another well-documented phenomenon. It is the classic midlife crisis, more aptly known as the U-shaped happiness curve. This researched theory is based on longitudinal experiments and global happiness data demonstrating greater life satisfaction prior to our thirties and after the age of fifty. Statistically, our least happy time is right around our midforties. In higher education, as in other industries, this is a time when our professional energy tends to be at its peak. Our careers may be flourishing, and we are fulfilling our personal and professional aspirations. It is also a time when we are solidly in the middle of our lives, many of us sandwiched between raising our kids and caring for our elders. We are juggling more responsibilities than we ever have in the past or will in the future as our lives simplify. We may be prone to societal messages of abundance—bigger house, nicer car, better office, more epic vacations, puffier title. And by the way, we are working in environments in service of young people, those for whom the future is wide open and the opportunities abundant. We get older while our target constituency does not. And this has the potential to make the bottom of the U-shaped happiness curve droop even lower.

Upper limit problems

Psychologist and author Gay Hendricks presents in his book *The Big Leap* four competence zones through which we manage our lives. The first he calls the Zone of Incompetence—we don't yet really know what we are doing. The second is the Zone of Competence—we can do the work and are beginning to hit our stride, though others perhaps can do it just as well. The third is the Zone of Excellence—we may be making a good living, but it is here where stagnation may arise. Hendricks describes this third zone as our most seductive and problematic. We may be comfortable and satisfied with our reputation, but we experience a nagging sense of withering. In a way, it all becomes too easy. On the surface, we may be doing well, but as Machiavelli noted, we "desire novelty to such an extent that those who are doing well wish for change as much as those doing badly." Hendricks describes a fourth and ultimate zone, called the Zone of Genius, representing our true stretch, that place where we push through what he calls upper limit problems, moving beyond comfort, satisfaction, and ego into something deeper, more challenging, and with greater risk and more substantial reward.

We witness upper limit problems time and time again on our campuses—the colleagues who stay in their roles a few years too long, the direct report who becomes so set in his routine that he disrupts legitimate attempts at innovation, or the divisional colleague who obsesses more over her retirement schedule than the work at hand. None of these are bad in and of themselves. But they can dampen progress. And for the colleagues in these roles, it can reduce their efficacy and satisfaction with their work. Tone setters don't freeze-frame the Zone of Excellence. They soften their edge of stagnation and look for ways to break out of its intoxicating grip and into the Zone of Genius.

Habit boredom

Even *Atomic Habits* author James Clear, weighs in on professional stagnation, suggesting that our "greatest threat to success is not failure but boredom." Honestly, not many of us, including my clients, are willing to admit we are bored at work. We are more apt to course correct, building walls of busyness around us, trying to solve stagnation with freneticism. If we were brutally honest with ourselves, we would admit that our focus becomes less about the strategic impact of a tone setter and more to carve out our territory. Clear adds, "We get bored with habits because they stop delighting us. The outcomes become expected. And as our habits become ordinary, we start derailing our progress to seek novelty."

We may not talk about it, but boredom is a real source of stagnation on our campuses. For so many of my clients, they point to a number of challenges. The most obvious is lack of promotional opportunities to keep work fresh. Another is the relentless drumbeat of the academic cycle as their source of stagnation, describing a slight dread around another incoming class, the next annual report, or the incoming president with the latest novel agenda. Also, the lack of campus activity during the summer does little to ease the nudge of stagnation. Those of us with twelve-month appointments are still expected to report to campus, even while it lacks the vibrant energy of the fall and spring semesters. Even dining services have shut down between May and September! Whatever your feelings around professional stagnation, there can be a fine line between boredom and outright cynicism.

Outdated success scripts

Think about how you ended up in your campus role. So often, what limits us in our journey to become tone setters is our inability to fully understand our backstory. We didn't get to our current administrative roles simply because of our SAT scores, our campus connections, or our dream of one day running a university. According to Mary Jacobsen in her seminal book *Hand-Me-Down Dreams*, our professional choices are largely the result of a tone set by our families and those who influenced us as we were growing up. For example, it is not lost on me that I have chosen a line of work that in some ways mimics my father's. As a college professor, he never came out and said to me that I should consider building my professional life around a college campus. Yet it's hard to ignore that I was influenced by his joy for his work—the students he would take on museum tours, the alumni who would return and share fond memories of Professor Ceperley, or the high-level meetings he would have with his president about the development of a new campus. There was a time when, after his college moved to a distant suburb, his commute became intolerable and he would sleep one night a week in his office on a cot he stored in a department storage closet.

Similarly, we have all come across students who were influenced by their parents' dreams and life choices. Think about the pre-med student who struggles to explain why she wishes to pursue a health career, except for the incredible pride her parents will possess once they have an MD in the family. Consider the first-generation political science major determined to ace the LSATs and gain admission to a top-ranked law school because his parents and teachers reminded him how good he was at arguing. Or how about the accounting major, driven by parental messaging like this: "If we are paying all this tuition, you are going to major in something practical that will land you a job when you graduate."

We can think of all these subtle and not-so-subtle messages as success scripts. When I work with higher education teams, I typically break them into three-person conversation pods to help them deepen their listening skills and provide them with opportunities to connect with one another, human to human. I ask them to reflect in their pods on the following questions inspired by the work of the Modern Elder Academy:

1. What were the scripts that were given to you when you were growing up?
2. Did you adopt these scripts, or did you rebel against them?
3. At what point in your life did an event happen that forced you to challenge your success script?
4. At what point did you develop a new success script?
5. From today on, what might be the new success script you would like to develop?

RUT MANAGEMENT

Even as esteemed higher education practitioners, we find ourselves in need of what I call rut management from time to time. Maybe it's just a dull sense that what used to get us pumped up no longer provides the same sizzle. As busy as we claim to be, inside we feel a professional emptiness. We are tumbling forward and may not know why or where we're going. Maybe for you it comes at the start of yet another semester with a different cast of characters but the same duties you have executed so many cycles before. Maybe it is the latest personnel challenge for which you would rather just kick the can down the road, hoping the toxic staff member will just resign. Maybe you are crashing down off a professional high that had you running on adrenaline, until now. Or maybe it is the limiting belief that you have topped out, peaked too soon, and have only a future of more of the same to look forward to.

OVERCOMING STAGNATION

Bay Area mindfulness guru and communication expert Oren Jay Sofer tells the story in a recent blog post of a conversation he had with his meditation teacher. "What can I hope to get from this practice?" Sofer asked. His teacher responded, "Nothing. This practice isn't about what you get. It's about what you let go of." Sofer may be onto something. So many causes of stagnation evoke an antidote of add-ons, more things that we can take on to scratch whatever itch is irritating us. And you and I have a history of success based on taking action. Our trajectory tracks perfectly with mainstream society. We are bombarded with messages of constant movement and the accumulation of a lot of physical and professional trinkets: wealth, promotion, fame, and other items of conspicuous consumption.

Our academies play right along with our *more, more, more* mentality. Consider the data we track on our graduates, paying close attention to prestige-building metrics: alumni starting salaries; admittance into top-ranked law and medical schools; and Fulbright, Truman, and Goldwater Award winners. At the same time, our development teams and presidents' offices aggressively court alumni who have achieved either fame or monetary success, ideally both. And our trustees, regents, and leadership boards typically comprise people in possession of significant social and financial capital. It all makes sense. Higher education at its core is about leveling up. It's about earning, obtaining, and leveraging once-in-a-lifetime experience. For those of us producing that experience, often behind the scenes, it can become difficult to provide the launchpad for others' skyrocketing success at a time when our career is sputtering.

Sometimes the best choice we can make is to pause and fully experience the gap. *Il dolce far niente* translates to "the sweetness of doing nothing." Tone setters find ways to honor the stillness, knowing that often in the pause comes the epiphany. We can use our professional plateaus on campus to be still, to reflect, and to regain our awareness that what we do, even when our motivation runs dry, does make a difference.

TONE SETTER MINDSETS

"Go where the energy is," said Elisabeth Kubler-Ross, who believed that grief and suffering might lead to a breakdown that allows us to become more human. "People are like stained-glass windows. They sparkle and shine when the sun is out, but when the darkness sets in, their true beauty is revealed only if there is a light from within." As tone setters, we can use our professional plateaus on campus to override the dullness of stagnation with the cleansing of stillness.

MINDSET #47

Benchmark.

Take your stagnation on the road as your schedule allows, visiting other schools and offices doing work like yours. Benchmarking is an excellent way to pick up inspiration and common ground from others. Giving others the opportunity to showcase their work is among the greatest gifts we can give others. It helps them articulate their stories, brag some on their accomplishments, and commiserate with you on shared challenges. And for you, it helps you strengthen existing relationships and initiate new ones while experiencing a campus environment that is unfamiliar.

MINDSET #48

Rethink your vacation.

Make your vacation more platonic, Plato-like (about learning). There is something refreshing about reading a job-related book while sunning by a pool. Or adding a few days of R & R on to your next conference. We seem to think that the best use of leave time is to completely disconnect. I respectfully disagree. Often, our most creative solutions to the campus problems that perplex us come when we are thousands of miles away from the day-to-day of campus life.

MINDSET #49

Refine something that has been backburnered.

Take inventory of those ideas you have had that you've not had the time or energy to implement. Sometimes when we have reached a plateau, it's time to explore what new things we might build. It might be a system enhancement, a new performance appraisal framework for your staff, a previously unexplored partnership. From stagnation can come a surprising burst of creative energy.

MINDSET #50

Join a campus committee. Better yet, lead one.

One of my bosses asked me to cochair a two-year task force to rewrite our university's overly punitive code of conduct. Although this was well outside my expertise, my colleague and I jumped in, gathering students, staff, faculty members, and provosts in twice monthly meetings about revisions to the code. Sometimes tedious but fascinating nonetheless, this experience upped my facilitation skills and introduced me to a highly nuanced side of student life to which I had limited exposure. I grew to understand and appreciate our discipline process, and I developed many new positive relationships.

MINDSET #51

Find a reason to stay connected with students.

I was once told by a committee member in an interview I was in for a leadership role on a new campus that I would have very little opportunity to meet with students if I were offered the job. At the time, I was more than ready to do less one-on-one student advising and took that remark as a gift. Two years later as I gained expertise in that role, I realized that I was losing touch with our industry's primary audience and along with it my purpose for the work. An *Anam Cara's* voice appeared in my head: "Don't forget the student." In whatever matter makes sense in your area, create opportunities to guarantee connection with students. For you, this may mean forming a student advisory group in your office or supervising a student intern, work-study employee, or graduate assistant. Or it may be simply taking a student to lunch once a month. It is always illuminating to be reminded of what it was like to be their age—anxious, excited, open, and full of anticipation.

MINDSET #52

Test the waters.

A longtime friend and colleague chose to answer the call of a higher education search firm and decided to apply for, and ultimately won, an exciting new role on a new campus. There was nothing wrong with his existing job. He had been doing it with much success for eight years, including through the pandemic, and was feeling open to what's next. He pursued the new role not to run away from anything but rather to make sense of his career path for a new audience. I have worked with as many people who have pursued jobs that did not land as his did, but the act of applying and interviewing gave them a fresh look at their existing roles. Just as importantly, they grew from being a candidate as they learned to effectively tell their stories.

POWERFUL QUESTION

What actions might you take to reignite your interest in your work?

CHAPTER 9

TRANSITION
Pursue the New

Without transition there is no air, no trick, no dazzling show. The transition provides the launch pad, and the landing, for all the fun stuff.

—Christine Sperber

C HANGING THINGS UP can be an antidote to stagnation, but many of us don't necessarily see it that way. Change is something to be avoided or put off. In the Greek myth of Icarus, the flying man was warned not to fly too close to the sun for fear his wings would melt. He did, and they did, and Icarus went crashing into the waves and died. According to Seth Godin in his book *The Icarus Deception*, too many of us have taken the fable to heart, staying far, far away from the rays of the sun, though perhaps to our detriment. Instead, we fly where we are comfortable, very close to the waves of the ocean. We hover, safe from the glare but held low by the lure of the water. Godin wonders if maybe there is a better place, in the middle between the sun and the surf. Right between the two is a zone of transition called the growth zone. This is a place of heightened attention, a bit of stress, and ultimately an expansion of our self-efficacy.

There is something freeing about exploring our zone of transition. Take a moment to reflect on your campus career thus far.

What major transitions have you pursued successfully?

What transitions have been thrust upon you?

Where are you right now? Are you in the zone of comfort, danger, or growth?

Many administrators I coach are trying to find their growth zone. They are either planning for a transition of their own (i.e., new role, new project, planned reorganization) or they are on the receiving end of transition (i.e., a change that was not initiated by them but that impacts their work nonetheless). In either scenario, transition can be challenging. Avoiding transition on our campuses is no longer an option. For those who think it is, Bette Davis summed up higher education's current reality in the movie *All About Eve* when she famously said, "Fasten your seatbelts; it's going to be a bumpy night." Let's explore higher education transition from two perspectives, the transitions you create and the disruptions to which you respond.

UNIVERSITY OF TEXAS

A white fluffy snow fell from the sky as the massive Mayflower moving truck growled to a stop in front of our Charlottesville, Virginia, home. Three hulky men wearing gloves and back braces emerged from the truck's cab and began a day-long effort of emptying our house and intricately scaffolding our furniture, dish packs, garment boxes, and even our car in the truck's cavernous cargo hold. Before the winter sun set, the men were done, and the truck pulled away bound for Texas.

Among the items rattling around in that truck was a single box representing my professional past. It was sealed tightly with packing tape, ANDY'S WORK STUFF scrawled in Sharpie on the top and two sides. Within the box were artifacts from the last chapter of my campus life— newsletters I wrote, publications I designed, a VHS tape of a student workshop I ran and of which I was especially proud, and a smattering of cards and mementos presented to me at my farewell party just days before.

Seven days later, the truck and the same three guys would arrive at our new apartment in Austin, Texas, on a much sunnier day surrounded by ubiquitous fields of bluebonnets and freeway signs that read DON'T MESS WITH TEXAS, a nod to the feisty and popular governor at the time, Ann Richards. All that was packed and stowed a week before in Virginia would need to be unpacked, box by box, so Skip and I could create a new home in a place where we knew no one. As has so often been the case in our careers, a college campus would provide an instant community for us to discover.

I was recruited by Dean Ellen Wartella to head up a small student services office in what is now the Moody College of Communication at the University of Texas. Ellen was a dynamic new dean at the time, eager to make her administrative mark as one of a small group of high-ranking female administrators on a campus known for its good-ol'-boy Texas ways and loyalty to an odd color on all its logo wear called Longhorn Orange. No one looks good in this color. No one!

But it is helpful to back up to the year before I met Dean Wartella because even then I had my eyes on Texas. From my steady job at the University of Virginia, I was growing restless. I was intrigued by UT-Austin's size, prominence, and oversize pride. Founded in 1883, the Lone Star State's flagship institution is home to eighteen colleges and schools, over three thousand faculty members, and a global alumni force of a half a million proud Texas Exes. Over fifty-two thousand students pack themselves into the university's dense forty-acre campus, and its College of Communication was the largest of its kind in the country.

Texas had turned me down, or should I say totally blew me off, for a job I believed was a perfect fit. Nearly a year passed before I came across the exact same job listing in the *Chronicle*. I dusted off the same résumé, cover letter, and reference list, and I applied ... again! I had nothing to lose, and this was an easy way to repurpose my application materials. The second time must have been a charm or my materials were mailed under a full moon or God wanted me at long last to work in an above-ground office. The chair of the search committee contacted me promptly, conducted a phone screen, and invited me to Austin for a site visit. Soon I found myself in my element, sitting with decision-makers in the college's Lady Bird Johnson Room surrounded by walls of photos of the former first lady, the only one in our nation's history to hold a degree in journalism (of course it was from Texas). A call came from the faculty member who was heading up the search. "Andy, you did great these last two days. Students, faculty, and the search committee are excited about your candidacy. You can be expecting an offer from the dean."

Could this be happening? I hung up the phone and stood in the window of my room at the Austin Marriott, the Spanish Renaissance–themed UT campus spreading out before me, its iconic tower bathed in orange to indicate a recent Longhorn win. How incredible to take on this new role in the great state of Texas and its techy, artistic, and deliciously funky capital. KEEP AUSTIN WEIRD! was a popular bumper sticker slapped on the backs of massive gas-guzzling Chevy Suburbans as they propelled up and down the two-level I-35 as it roared by the university.

In truth, and I firmly believe this, I was meant to remain in Charlottesville for another year for two reasons. The first was to be close to my mother, who passed away at sixty-seven from Creutzfeldt-Jakob disease. The second was to audition and be cast in a small community theater production of the musical *Evita* and to meet someone in the cast named Skip who was to become my dearest friend, my partner, my husband, and my beloved to this day. Call it wacky superstition, but I believe it was these two things that foiled my first attempt at a move to the Lone Star State.

LIMINALITY

As the moving truck pulled up to our new apartment on Metric Boulevard in North Austin, Skip and I experienced this surreal state of living fully in between. Perhaps you can relate to those times when you have relished the sweet spot between administrative roles you've played or campuses you have served. It is a time to be explored, enjoyed, even cherished. I remember sitting on the floor of our balcony, watching our first spectacular Texas sunset. Father Richard Rohr refers to times like this as "liminal spaces," where in his words "we are betwixt and between the familiar and the completely unknown. There alone is our old world left behind, while we are not yet sure of the new existence.

That's a good space where genuine newness can begin." Our campuses afford us beautiful endings and clean new beginnings as administrators, just as they did when we were college students. And when we are orchestrating the transition, as I was when we moved to Texas, the sense of pride and ownership is palpable.

Any kind of transition we make in higher education positions us as the protagonist of a story, one that rarely turns out as we expected but one that nonetheless is a page turner, plopping us right in the growth zone. Noted mythologist Joseph Campbell figured this out when he popularized the idea of the hero's journey in his 1949 book, *The Hero with a Thousand Faces*. Campbell argued that every story follows a common narrative, even mine when I left Charlottesville and built a new life in Austin. Stories always have three beats. First is a *departure*, where a challenge surfaces and the protagonist must rise to the occasion. Next comes an *initiation*, where they face trials and question if it is all worth it. Finally, our resilient protagonist *returns* from the journey—tested, wise, and better for having survived it.

Dr. William Bridges in his best-selling book *Managing Transitions* builds on the narrative metaphor to help leaders navigate a quickly changing landscape. He, too, suggests three beats, or phases as he calls them. Beat 1 is the ending, the loss, the letting go. Beat 2 is the neutral or the "not knowing" zone. Beat 3 is the new beginning. For both Campbell and Bridges, life's richness comes right in the middle, in the initiation, the not-knowing zone, the second beat of the narrative. Although my self-determined transition did not bring me back to the University of Virginia as Campbell might predict, it did track perfectly with the various parts of the hero's journey, and it certainly mapped with Bridges's three phases of transition.

The ability to sink into liminality ranks high among the enviable characteristics of tone setters. Like you and me, they have attended more than their share of conferences addressing the increasing rapidity of change. And they have transitioned time and time again as professionals. Somehow, they seem to effortlessly roll with it—all the interim roles, new initiatives, special projects, and countless "service to the community" roles that fill their plates and give them something fresh on which to make their mark. For them, regular transition is a gift. But tone setters exit knowing that what they did, while they were in place, caught fire and made a difference.

LOYOLA MARYMOUNT UNIVERSITY

It is one thing to experience transition in the growth zone when we are feeling empowered to orchestrate change. It is quite another when transition feels more like disruption. I found myself leading in the midst of disruption early on in my consulting career. I was invited to pursue a project that allowed me to "sit down" on a campus for the better part of an entire academic year at Loyola Marymount University in Los Angeles. I was hired by Dr. Maureen Weatherall, a dynamic vice provost, to serve as the fixed-term in-between guy, implementing the early stages of an organizational shift that split a student-facing office in two while shifting its reporting structure from one division to another.

The opportunity for me was optimal at the time, as was the cozy furnished penthouse apartment I rented with a view of the Santa Monica Pier and its surrounding expanse of sandy beach lining the Pacific Ocean. My daily commute to campus took me along Lincoln Boulevard, passing through beachy hipster grunge hot spots like Venice and Abbott Kinney before waving to the attendant in LMU's entrance kiosk and climbing the curving steep hillside road to the university's main campus, the "bluff" as it's called by LMU Lions.

From atop that bluff was a depiction of the ultimate Los Angeles postcard. Once parked, I would walk through the sunken gardens by the Sacred Heart Chapel. The panorama was breathtaking—from the growth of Playa Vista's burgeoning Silicon Beach below to the jets stacked up in their landing pattern into LAX to the south, the bobbing yachts tethered to their docks in Marina del Rey to the west, the skyline of Westwood and the Getty Museum to the north, and to the sprawl of Hollywood to the east and its iconic sign on the hill above. By simply rotating my head from this magical vantage point on the LMU bluff, I could see it all, the City of Angels spread out before me. *Princeton Review* recently ranked LMU among the top five most beautiful campuses in the country. I could understand why.

So it's odd to think that LMU's spectacular campus could possibly be a place of higher education disruption. After all, a community of Catholic priests live on that bluff. Their steady presence evokes the traditional values of St. Ignatius of Loyola, a sixteenth-century soldier turned mystic who created the Society of Jesus to help humanity find a "way of proceeding" to lives of greater fulfillment. According to popular Jesuit author James Martin in *The Jesuit Guide to (Almost) Everything*, the Jesuits are known for their work ethic and getting things done. Father Martin tells the story of a Franciscan, a Dominican, and a Jesuit celebrating mass together when the lights suddenly go out in the church. The Franciscan praises the chance to live more simply. The Dominican delivers a studious homily of how God brings light to the world. The Jesuit goes to the basement to fix the fuses.

And so it went at practical, faith-based, Loyola Marymount University, considered to be an up-and-coming underdog in a city fixated on the selectivity of UCLA and the feverish loyalty of USC Trojans. LMU is among the twenty-eight Jesuit colleges and universities in the United States, and there are some 189 Jesuit institutions of higher learning throughout the world. All of them are grounded in the education of the whole student, exposing learners to issues of social justice, power and privilege, and student *vocare* retreats of reflection and renewal. One need not identify as Catholic to feel a sense of belonging here. Many Jesuit schools, including LMU, are now led by strong lay presidents instead of priests. Students designating "Catholic" as their faith tradition in campus surveys now account for less than 50 percent of Catholic school enrollments, and many identify themselves as more "spiritual" than "religious." Long-standing Catholic college metrics such as number of theology classes and daily mass attendance are being subsumed by topics of broader interest to campus communities, such as "how to lead a better life." In fact, LMU offers a degree in yoga studies.

As quintessentially picture-perfect as LMU appears, it walks a balance beam between a traditional residential college campus and a cutting-edge learning factory, producing graduates who excel in business, education, engineering, film, and law. Although no senior administrator ever said to me, "Andy, we brought you in to disrupt," I was recruited to even out the experience of change for those staff members most affected by it. The provost's division was being reshuffled, and the office I helped reposition was leaving its former home in the student affairs division and moving to a new, more strategic placement in the enrollment management division—alongside admissions, financial aid, and the registrar. Although in some ways this appeared to be little more than shifts in reporting structure and funding allocations, for those whose professional identities were rooted in the way things were, the reorganization brought about anxiety, gossip, and in some cases entrenchment among those most impacted. Saying to a staff member on a campus, "It's just business," lands just about as well as telling them you are planning to remove one of their limbs. People get stuck in the sentimental ideas they have about the academy, and the suggestion of change, even if well-intentioned which it almost always is, can be viewed as a threat.

My LMU experience and my UT-Austin experience both taught me about change, but the lessons learned were vastly different. Moving from Virginia to Texas to take on my dream job was a transition I created. I saw a prize, and I went after it. At LMU, I was tasked with facilitating a change I did not invent and working with well intentioned people whose response to change ran the gamut from enthusiasm to resistance.

EVIDENCE OF MASSIVE CHANGE

Higher education journalist Jeff Selingo coauthored a recent report with Deloitte that offers a stark foreshadowing of our campus landscapes of the future. Change is in the air, and not always where you and I might expect it. Whereas we built college campuses that run like small cities, we didn't forecast what they would feel like if void of the life and energy of students, faculty, and staff. How do we set a tone in a place with a thick tension between a 24-7, full-on site campus and a talent pool for whom over 50 percent are looking to switch jobs?

The College and University Professional Association for Human Resources (CUPA-HR) finds that whereas pay drives nearly 75 percent of administrative job seekers into search mode, 42 percent are now motivated by the flexibility that comes with remote work arrangements. That's nearly half! The report goes on to state, "Both faculty and staff want colleges to stop making them choose between a commitment to students and their own careers and needs of their families." Further, our campus C-suites have become revolving doors where presidential turnover continues at an unprecedented rate. We can no longer assume that our staff is willing to spend forty-plus hours per week in an office on campus. Maybe we are not either. As a client shared with me in a recent coaching session, "Andy, I've had it. I am quitting my current 4/1 and have taken I a job that offers me a 3/2," referencing an increasingly relevant fraction measuring the number of days on campus and the number of days working remotely.

How Change is Playing Out

To become more nimble, more efficient, and more budget-sensitive, I offer five disruptive practices that tone setters need to navigate within.

Shared services

Organizational empire building on our campuses is becoming a thing of the past. Where at one time an administrative office might have its own business officer, webmaster, marketing coordinator, and HR representatives, those roles—often well paid—are being centralized at the divisional level.

Interim appointments

Staffing our administrative ranks has become a chess game. From program coordinators to directors, deans, and presidents—college and university organizational charts today are filled with professionals keeping seats warm on an acting basis.

Fixed-term contracts

There is a compelling business case to place certain roles on fixed terms, typically one to three years.

Open concept offices

Other countries are decades ahead of the United States in breaking down walls and recreating workspaces for an ever-shifting workforce.

Dual reporting

Org charts are evolving too. We are seeing more "dotted-line" structures, where an administrator reports to two leaders, sometimes a faculty and staff leader, and sometimes, as in the case of development, to an academic dean and a senior staff member.

When Disruption Leaves You on the Outside

So far, I've placed us in the driver's seat of transformative change (a.k.a. disruption). But sometimes even the savviest of tone setters might find themselves on the outside of change plans. It may be that a planning group has formed and you are not part of the initial meetings. Or a reorganization is announced, and your position is on the chopping block for elimination. Sometimes, unbeknownst to us in the middle, a new leader is brought in to shake things up, and we become viewed, whether fairly or not, as the old guard that needs to be "repurposed." This has happened to many I've coached. Make no mistake, especially if you take pride in your work and feel confident in the tone you set on campus, being left out of significant change hurts. For some, it hurts quite deeply. It's personal, even if every self-help book tries to tell us it's not.

Higher education is changing at an increasingly rapid pace, though it may not always feel that way. As tone setters, we are changing as well. For every situational change we face—taking an exciting new job, navigating a challenging reorganization, or considering life beyond the academy—we deal with the psychological effects prompted by the change. Our real limitations may rear their ugly heads. We may experience fear. We may wonder how change will intersect with our values and professional purpose. Is it time for us to move up? Perhaps we need to move out. It's all too easy to let all the unknowns in our future freeze us in place.

Or we can leverage the mindsets we've mastered to pursue with all our might all the growth that stems from these transitions. Our industry's movement into the future creates ample possibility for resourceful tone setters. There are always things to be cleaned up, reorganized, reinvigorated, and even disrupted. As our wisdom crystallizes, we become more adept at predicting and sailing through inevitable transition, on our own terms. We learn how to be the new kids and move into our new organizational neighborhood with grace. We learn how to play new roles within our institutions, leveraging moments when we can step in and make impact. And perhaps most importantly, we unleash our powerful intuition and decide when it is time to go—onto a new role, to a new campus, or to a new life chapter.

Seizing the Moment

Bringing about significant change requires a deep level of intuition and a willingness to seize the moment. As I often share with my coaching clients who have reached roadblocks in their drive for impact, "A response of No today does not mean an idea is permanently off the table." Transformative disruption can only happen if the climate for change is optimal. We need the ideal mix of enthusiastic leadership and staff, guaranteed financial resources, and a clear outcome (e.g., more efficient processes, better student experiences, etc.). A terrific idea you might have for curriculum enhancement under your current president may gain no traction, whereas under a future president it might be considered a stroke of brilliance. Or this year's drop in freshman enrollment may lead to cost-cutting measures that put the kibosh on a technology enhancement your team has started working on. In the future, a donor may appear seemingly out of thin air who is excited about funding your innovation. As a tone setter, you need to be persistent, watching and waiting for the magic alchemy of strategy, money, and people to launch you into the incredibly rewarding and needed work of innovation.

FOR THE LOVE OF TRANSITION

If you haven't figured it out already, I am a change junkie. I like it. I believe it keeps me fresh, on my toes, just a tad in over my head most of the time. I believe the campus tone setters we know would nod approvingly. Remember, unlike our tenured faculty colleagues, we in the administrative core have nothing resembling rank or tenure. There are few, if any, ladders for us to climb. We don't rise from assistant professor to associate professor to full professor. So we must creatively build our career, one gig at a time. When we resist change, in most cases it doesn't serve us. Instead, change happens all around us, and there we sit, unchanged in an environment that has moved on. Tone setters ride the waves of change, whether through their invention or their responses to inevitable disruption. And let's be honest—that feels very, very good. We like to be noticed for the right reasons and invited to tables where we never imagined we would feast.

The question is, what do we do with these opportunities? Who do we become by pursuing them, especially those that take us places we never imagined? Do these pursuits make us smarter? Maybe. Do they make us wiser? Absolutely! But only if we allow them to transform us.

Tone setters are gifted at cascading in changes in a manner that engages most everyone who needs to be engaged. They lean into discussions of massive innovation, and as they do, they consider the cost-benefit of their proposal. They see an end game that creates an improved program, refined process, or higher level of services. And they know that there will be those who may disagree vociferously, even attempting to sabotage change efforts. But tone setters ignite their creativity, bringing the outliers in to the solution rather than leaving them on the periphery to stew. They pursue a change process calculating the cost of the negative energy and ensuring that it is outweighed by the positive impact.

Tone Setter Mindsets

As a tone setter, I want you to not only understand disruption but to see the value in generating transformative disruption and responding optimally to disruption not of your making—to enhance your campus in a manner that only you can. You will find yourself both in a position of leading change and being the recipient of change you did not invent.

Mindset #53
Manage the change narrative.
With disruptive change comes a deluge of speculation. There is noise everywhere. If you are leading change, be relentless in sharing uplifting communications that describe a current reality, track publicly the steps to an improved reality, and create affirming milestones and celebrations to demonstrate momentum. Choose your words carefully, and continue to track subtle and not-so-subtle feedback from those most impacted.

Mindset #54
Increase staff engagement with tiger teams.
Our campuses are all about shared governance. We bring community members together for myriad reasons: to plan graduation, to interview candidates, to develop a strategic plan, and to manage crisis. Many of these gatherings are fixed term. They have a beginning, and they have a concluding deliverable. Consider using this model for smaller problems you are trying to solve in your area. Bring together a small fast-acting tiger team (usually four or five people), assign a chair whom you are looking to develop as a leader, and craft a clear set of expected deliverables to guide their work. Select people for whom you will like to

create a shared experience, colleagues who have a skill or an interest in the area of concern and would benefit from the accomplishment that a tiger team might bring.

MINDSET #55

Lean on your intuition.

Wherever you are in your liminal space—before, during, or after a shift—pay close attention to your gut. Consider what needs to change, whether it be your attitude or your circumstances. If you are a lame duck, consider the positive impact you can make before you depart. If you have started a new role, consider how you engage with others during this important time of first impressions. And if you are in the messy middle, soak it up with relish because it marks a rare and tremendous period of rejuvenation and wide-open space.

MINDSET #56

Create space for your successor.

After you have left your role, trust that the organization will survive without you. Eventually, your successor will be named, and you want to give that individual the chance to set their own unique tone. You can offer to be available for support if that feels comfortable, but you don't want to be meddlesome to a leader who ultimately needs to find the best path forward. You also don't want to be visibly hanging around with your old gang, comparing notes that drift into gossip about the new professional. The new path may be similar to the path you forged before, or it may be entirely different. You did your good work. Now it's time to let the next person do theirs.

MINDSET #57

Reach out to your predecessor.

Just as important as it is to celebrate the continued evolution of the campus organization you supported, it is equally valuable for you to initiate a friendly check-in with the professional you succeed. Often, we get swept into new roles with reasonable fanfare and not infrequent demonization of the previous administrator in our seat. "Thank God you are here!" colleagues may chant. But be careful of becoming too cozy with a savior complex. Your predecessor may likely have some helpful insights about the campus and its politics. Even if shared through a bitter lens, there are nuggets of insight that can help you. Plus, that person will surely appreciate your outreach.

MINDSET #58

Consider your legacy.

Think of your transition as a eulogy builder, not a résumé enhancer. You may be part of something that will make a substantial impact on the student experience. Recognize that you always leave something of value behind. Count on it. It might be a new procedure, an innovative program, fiscal stability, or talent we recruited that go on to flourish. It could be legions of other value adds. You may or may not be credited for them.

MINDSET #59

Engage at the highest level possible to see the big picture.

Rather than simply reacting to changes that were not of our making, a helpful tone setter mindset is to pursue understanding of the change. Try to get curious as to why, from the perspective of those at a higher level, the proposed disruption is advantageous for the campus. Could it be a cost-saving measure? Or a need to centralize services for efficiency? Maybe there is a donor whose philanthropy is dependent on an organizational shift. I am not saying that any of this is fair or even strategic, but as a tone setter, you need to do what it takes to bypass victimhood and understand the why of change.

MINDSET #60

Remain flexible and open to change, growth, and evolution.

As Lao Tzu put it: "Whoever is soft and yielding is a disciple of life. The hard and stiff will be broken. The soft and supple will prevail." Try to get comfortable with the inevitability of change and neutralize it, embracing that it may be neither good nor bad but that it is a facet of any organization, and in most cases over time change results in a positive outcome, maybe not right away but eventually.

POWERFUL QUESTION

How will you experience your next campus transition in the growth zone?

PART FOUR

Accessing Your Wisdom

I AM KNOWN TO ask my coaching clients who feel stuck in the middle of their university careers, "What will it take for you to become a wisdom worker?" They often like the way that question sounds, even if they're not sure how best to answer it.

Wisdom, it turns out, comes not from the accumulation of more knowledge but from a shift in how we utilize all the knowledge we have gained. Arthur Brooks writes in his book *From Strength to Strength* that our intelligence naturally evolves over time from a fluid intelligence—developing new knowledge and skills to perform more optimally, a.k.a. getting smarter—to a crystallized intelligence, where we continue to learn while we expend more mental and creative energy on integration and assimilation. In essence, we fuse together all our experiences—the skill development, the successes, the limitations overcome, the transitions—and ultimately we grow our wisdom. We level up from being tone setters to becoming wise tone setters. That explains how we grow from a scheduling assistant at our university to successfully managing an entire registrar's office or from a fundraising coordinator to a highly regarded major gifts officer. We learn the specific skills to do a direct service job, and we build on them. We pick up other skills, eventually integrating all of them into a more detailed map from which to navigate.

So, what is this wisdom thing, and how do we see it in our campus tone setters while cultivating it in ourselves? The cultivation of wisdom is not a guaranteed outcome, even after years of experience. It's not a rite of passage that comes with age. Higher education elders can be wise, sure, but so can administrators much earlier on in their careers. Wisdom is about connected dots and making sense of the disparate aspects of our campus lives.

Let's complete our understanding of *Tone Setters in the Academy* by distilling all that we have discovered into six pillars of wisdom.

CHAPTER 10

PILLARS OF CHARACTER WISDOM

To want what you have, and to not want what you don't have, is the beginning of wisdom.

—Jack Kornfield

S O FAR, WE have examined our capacity as tone setters through three lenses. We looked at how we can cultivate our tone on campus in Part One, how we can manage our energy for the long stretch in Part Two, and how we can go about softening our edges in Part Three. Throughout, I have introduced tone setter mindsets to provide you with tangible, actionable options for you to consider. Now it's time to integrate all the ingredients into a broader framework, or what I call the six pillars of wisdom. In this chapter we will examine the first three pillars of character wisdom, and in the next chapter we will look at the three pillars of reputational wisdom.

Former monk and best-selling author Jay Shetty writes, "You can't be anything you want, but you can be everything you are." Accessing this "everything" is what coaching is all about. The Co-Active Training Institute (CTI) is among the largest coaches' training schools in the world. As one of their graduates, I use one of their cornerstones with all my university clients. It's simple, and it starts with an assumption that we are all NCRW—naturally creative, resourceful, and whole. You start with abundance, not deficit. You have everything you need to step up to the challenges and opportunities that lie ahead. You just need to tap it. This is the ultimate calling of tone setters.

A School at the End of a Dirt Road

The topic of wisdom was on my mind as sixteen of us sat on yoga cushions, legs crossed, in a semicircle, on a vast deck high above the beach below, watching in anticipation as the deep orange sun dropped slowly into the ocean. The waves crashed loudly, exploding in a roar and an otherworldly crackling as they stirred up the rocks that cluttered the shore, nature's outcome from a hurricane a few weeks before. All of us were motionless, except for the regular batting of flies from around our faces as the humidity of the day gave way to a subtle evening breeze.

Our facilitator was a tattooed sexagenarian with a shock of white blond hair kissed by decades of sun and skateboarding. He sat on the edge of the deck, back to the ocean, facing us, the three big dogs that seemed to follow him everywhere lounging at his side. He welcomed us to the Modern Elder Academy with a prompt for reflection and sharing, asking, "Would each of you introduce yourself and share what you would like to gain in the week ahead?" One by one, voices rose up from around the circle.

"To find inner peace," shared one.

"To get to a place of clarity," offered another.

"To come to terms with a personal transition I am facing," volunteered a third.

Each intention expressed was met with a nod of approval from our host and warm smiles of knowingness from the others. That is, until it was my turn.

"I am here working on a book, and I would like to complete drafts of my first three chapters," I boomed with the pride of productivity.

Then there was silence, except for the deafening sound of the crashing waves. Did I miss a cue? Apparently, I did. It was as if our host lifted my intention from my lips and used it as an example of what not to do.

"It's important to become comfortable with stillness," he said. "We are not human doings; we are human beings. This is a place to rest, refresh, and be still."

I guess he was onto something.

The Modern Elder Academy was a campus like none I had ever seen. There are no degrees to be earned, no tenured faculty in classrooms, and no eighteen-to-twenty-two-year-olds filling the place with the adrenaline of early adulthood. This place was different. It took my driver seventy-five minutes to travel north from the Los Cabos San Jose Airport to the campus, a self-identified wisdom school in Baja, California Sur, Mexico. The ride was easy and scenic along a stretch of new highway until the final mile, which consisted of rutted dirt roads that tossed me from side to side in the back of the black sport utility.

When we finally pulled up in front of a nondescript collection of stucco buildings, I peered through the window as a young man opened the car door and leaned in with an enthusiastic "Welcome, Andrew, to Modern Elder Academy! I'm Jonathan." I laughed, remembering the opening line from one of my childhood nighttime soaps: "Welcome to Fantasy Island!" Jonathan then grabbed my suitcase, hailed the driver away in a cloud of dust, and led me through a gate into a leafy entrance courtyard. Together we began my orientation to MEA—wandering down terra cotta paths, across contemplative terraces, around dipping pools, and eventually stopping at what was to be my private casita for the next two weeks.

MEA was a campus of a different sort. Self-identified as a wisdom school, the grounds were a cluster of haciendas with cozy sleeping rooms intermingled with swimming pools, outdoor lounges and firepits, a serene carpeted classroom with comfy chairs and cushions, a glass-encased yoga studio, and even a working farm. MEA's Sabbatical Session, or "Sabsesh" to its alumni, provided the perfect environment for me to put the finishing touches on my book outline and get to work on my early chapters in preparation for my first looming manuscript deadline. Stillness be damned!

In between writing sessions on my MacBook Air, I could join other Sabseshers in many of MEA's amenities, including sound baths and massage, facilitated conversations with mindfulness practitioners, artfully prepared meals on the oceanfront terrace, and several kitchens stocked with snacks, beverages, and those addictive chocolate-covered almonds (you can buy them at Costco!). Margaritas were prepared upon request by a friendly mixologist. There was even a shaman who was available by appointment to read our energies.

PILLARS OF CHARACTER WISDOM

What if we could bottle up all of our tone setter mindsets into characteristics, both discrete and public, that fully demonstrate our ultimate tone as college and university administrators? My mini sabbatical at MEA provided an ideal setting to reflect on what is within reach for all of us, growing superpowers that guide our movements without the pressure of self-promotion. Development of our character wisdom is an inside game, shaped from all we experience, good and bad. Character wisdom isn't something that we do. It's more like our strong foundation. Looking at the image, we can think of our character wisdom pillars as three pillars that strengthen our foundation, grounding us to the earth through our presence, our perspective, and our equanimity.

Pillar of Presence

Campus tone setters are fully experiencing this moment in time. They have learned from the past, and they have a vision for the future. But right now, tone setters exhibit alertness, curiosity, and intentionality. They are alert to the scene before them, without the distractions so commonplace on our busy campuses today. Think of those you know on your campus who seem adept at being fully engaged at meetings. Can you picture your colleague who you know is reading the room, paying attention to all the visible and not-so-visible cues of behavior among their peers? When we are in the presence of people like this, we experience that all-too-uncommon satisfaction of being seen and heard. Tone setters who exhibit presence create space for the engagement of others. When they are not speaking, they are watching, absorbing, and processing—not with the eye of a critic or chomping at the bit to jump in but with a spirit of someone who wants to learn more.

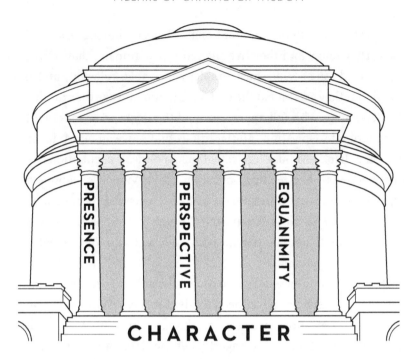

PRESENCE PERSPECTIVE EQUANIMITY

CHARACTER

Second, tone setters are genuinely curious. In a recent coach training I attended, each of us in the cohort was asked to share a photograph of ourselves taken when we were about five years of age and to have it in front of us during a reflection exercise. My photo was super adorable, if I do say so. There I was, dressed in overalls, standing in my yard in front of my mother's marigolds. "What was it like," our facilitator asked, "to be that age, where we made few if any assumptions, where we could find interest in almost anything?" I thought about the pot of soup on the stove when my mother lit the gas burner (a spaceship taking off), sidewalks in my neighborhood (the roads I traveled on my bike to get to my very adult pretend job), and our basement filled with my grandmother's china (my pretend home where I would entertain my fictional friends at lavish parties). Chip Conley writes, "To have a young spirit means that we aren't jaded by the reality and harshness of life. We're still wide-eyed and awestruck by the miraculous and influenced by the mystical and unexplainable." Such curiosity goes a long way for wise tone setters.

Third, tone setters are intentional. They set, pursue, and achieve goals. They know and they live the SMART acronym—that what they set out to do is specific, measurable, achievable, relevant, and time-bound. But they add an *I* at the end for intentionality as they fulfill their SMART-I goals with full appreciation of the micro moments that lead to the ultimate aspiration. All the rituals that move an effort down the field—the back-of-house conversations, political negotiations, planning meetings, cheerleading, and even the inevitable misunderstandings—these are what ultimately lead to the intended future state, the goal. And these rituals are managed through intentions, a resolve or a determination to act in a certain way. They focus on the current state, not just on the outcome.

Even for our tone setters who model the pillar of presence, this wisdom characteristic has never been harder to access. With smartphones or laptops often in our hands or on the table in front of us, we have plenty of distraction at our fingertips—from data and news to advice. We call it multitasking, and we claim it as if it were a superpower. But here's the thing. When tone setters are engaging us, their phones are rarely visible, their ears are not plugged with alien-looking ear buds, and their eyes are not shuffling through papers or scrolling through email. Their attention, curiosity, and intention are fixated on us. They are liberated, untethered by stuff. As a coaching client of mine wisely said about his quest for hands-free presence, "I want the most important person to be the person who is right in front of me right now."

At a recent meeting with Amy Johnson, vice chancellor of student affairs at University of North Carolina's Chapel Hill, I marveled at how she broke the ice for our 4:00 p.m. chat in her comfortable office in the Henry Owl building, named for UNC's first Native American student. Her day, as she described, was dense with meetings, difficult negotiations, parent fires to put out, and student discipline cases to resolve. And then she said, "And, Andy, tell me about your day." That prompt led to a lively free-flowing conversation about the consulting work I was doing there. It was the most beautiful two-way conversation, and when it ended forty-five minutes later, I felt like we had covered some important ground and enjoyed ourselves as we were doing it. There were no phones to answer, no email to check, no knock on the door to usher me out. It was the flow of pure attention.

Pillar of Perspective

Question: How many ways do our tone setters approach a problem? Answer: As many as it takes to land on an optimal solution. Our campus careers have a ton of problems to be solved: resource problems, workload problems, political problems, systems problems. Tone setters fly over problems with the eye of a helicopter pilot on a rescue mission. All the issues on the ground below are part of the scenery. They are neither good nor bad. Problems are neutral. They are inevitable. Perspective acts as the compass guiding decisions, actions, and interactions, and wise tone setters applying this pillar see beyond the immediate circumstances and grasp the broader context.

The more complex our campus problems become, the more elaborate our decision-making needs to become. Often, it might seem efficient to go with our hunch. There is nothing wrong with channeling our intuition. But the best decisions when the stakes really matter go beyond merely confirming a suspicion or hunch. Adam Grant writes, "Confirmation bias is dismissing inconvenient facts. Critical thinking is questioning your beliefs. The goal of learning is to pursue what's true, not defend your views." Grant is describing the importance of well-reasoned response over hasty reaction in order to clear our desks and move on. Tone setters don't run from the complexities of institutional circumstance hoping to beat traffic on Friday afternoon. Rather, they pursue multiple approaches to any situation they face, and they establish a best scenario path forward only after exploring a variety of perspectives.

One student life director I worked with recently was challenged by a common people problem: a disgruntled employee (we will call him Sam) who was missing deadlines, showing up late, and exhibiting a poor attitude. My client happened to have a whiteboard in her office, and I asked her to face the camera so I could see the board. Then I asked her to grab a dry erase marker and write in large letters in the middle of the board the name of the problem she wished to solve. She selected a green marker and in bold block letters wrote, "Sam's Work Performance." Then I asked her to draw a circle around "Sam's Work Performance" and to back up from the board and look closely at what she had written. What's not currently visible about Sam's work performance that appears above the circle? What about below? To the left and the right? Then I asked, "How many different ways do you think we might explore this problem?"

"I don't know," she replied. "Maybe six?"

"Great!" I said. "Let's see if we can discover six different perspectives on this problem, and I'd like you to write each of them on the board around the circle in a different color."

She looked at me blankly. "Give it a minute or two," I said. "Think about the different ways you can create an environment in which this problem resolves itself."

"Well," she admitted. "Sam is a new father, and he and his partner have not been sleeping well since their daughter was born."

"OK," I said. "Pick a different color marker and write 'New Parent' somewhere around the circle."

"What's another perspective?" I asked.

"Our admin and some of Sam's peers are needing to pick up his slack, and they are starting to gripe about it."

"Nice," I said. "Pick another color and write 'Impact on Peers' somewhere else around the circle."

Within a few minutes Sam's director had a colorful group of perspectives surrounding "Sam's Work Performance," including "Being Underemployed," "Solitary Work Style," "Dated Job Description," and "Getting on My Last Nerve" (this last one was just for fun).

I then asked her to pick the perspective that had the most juice, the one that really resonated with her. She quickly determined that there was a perspective between Sam's underemployment and his dated job description that was worth exploring. She underlined both of them in black. In fact, his current performance challenges had less to do with his natural exhaustion as a new father and more to do with the need to pursue greater challenges and fill gaps not yet addressed in her changing organization. The director was able to develop a strategy to support Sam, and her team, by revising Sam's position description to challenge him in new ways while filling programmatic gaps in her office. She moved into action only after an examination of feasible perspectives and the resulting clarity that comes from the solution path with the greatest resonance.

This is one illustration of the perspective pillar and a reminder that higher education tone setters can make the best decisions when they have all the information available.

Pillar of Equanimity

Equanimity describes a state of mental balance and even-mindedness. We might think of it as rolling with the punches or leaning into the inevitable ups and downs of our higher education careers. This character pillar asks us to walk a middle path, the path between cool, confident, no-drama steadiness and the path of exploration, adventure, and measured risk. Equanimity is an unwavering composure amid turmoil.

I can remember vividly a massive protest at UC San Diego that resulted from a racist fraternity party that quickly went viral, catching the attention of the national media and pushing the university's senior administration and communications staff into crisis management and damage control. The buildings housing the chancellor and senior administration were locked down, leaving our highest-level officials without offices during the upheaval. One of those was Vice Chancellor Penny Rue, my boss at the time and a tone setter case study in equanimity. As I welcomed Penny and others on her core team in my building to get them away from the chanting crowds, she demonstrated this surreal coolness as she went about the critical work of ensuring the safety of twenty-nine thousand UCSD students, advising the chancellor, her boss, and working with university communications on an appropriate response for the media.

Penny demonstrated a kind of stoicism. Like the ancient Greeks and Romans, from whom the term generated, playing a central role in the de-escalation of the protests while keeping her wits about her, keeping it light, and treating it almost as if it was all in a day's work. We see this time and time again with our most senior campus tone setters—whether calming an outraged mass of students or delivering the tragic news to the family of a student who passed away, they manage to do the work.

It is difficult when we pour much of our psychological and emotional energy into our work, and as an industry, higher education is effective at drawing us in and securing our commitment. Yet if we are truly as wise as our tone setters, we become skilled about placing our campus personas in a container and pursue expansive lives both within and outside that container. Tone setters get very good at maintaining an air of nonattachment. They roll along. They move ahead. They pick themselves up from disappointment and focus on the work of today and the opportunities of tomorrow.

For instance, suppose an enrollment decline on your campus requires you to reduce next year's operational budget by 20 percent. When you first hear the news, you might muse that the cut will become permanent, that it is pervasive throughout your institution, and that somehow it speaks to a weakness in your leadership. Somehow, it is personal, and somehow the sky is falling. On the other hand, the wise tone setter in you counters that negativity with a more realistic perspective on the circumstance. The 20 percent cut is a temporary solution, and finances will improve over time. This reduction is not happening everywhere, nor does it foreshadow some ultimate doomsday.

Cementing Our Foundation

Tone setters' ability to be present, to explore perspectives, and to act with equanimity give them a kind of invisible strength. These pillars aren't sparkle ponies for all to admire. Tone setters don't leverage them to impress people. Rather, pillars of character wisdom serve as a kind of operating system on which our campus tone setters rely. For me, a job disappointment at Stanford did not suddenly make me wise. What it did was grow my capacity to be present on campus, to explore the many perspectives to things that needed fixing, and to roll through the ups and downs with equanimity.

CHAPTER 11

PILLARS OF REPUTATIONAL WISDOM

I have one life and one chance to make it count for something.

—JIMMY CARTER

I N THE LAST chapter, we began to explore tone setters' most compelling character wisdom principles. Although the quest for wisdom may appear baked into the intellectual rigor of our campuses, it expands well beyond our academic pedigrees and professional titles. It's a muscle to be developed by all of us, regardless of our age, years of service, or pay grade. Wisdom, both in its private state and in its public manifestation, as will be explored in this chapter, is a quiet "credential," and it propels us as campus professionals without much ta-da or self-congratulation. Wisdom is agnostic to age, reputation, title, and years of service on campus. It advances the meaning and impact of our work, free of self-congratulation and epic mic drops. Your campus experience affords you countless opportunities to grow your reputational wisdom.

NEW ERA SCHOOLS OF WISDOM

It turns out that the Modern Elder Academy described in the last chapter is on the cutting edge of a new facet of higher learning. Described as a wisdom school for people in their middlescence, MEA is a cross between a new age retreat center, like Esalen, and a finely appointed hotel; picture a Ritz-Carlton. I've never been one for yurt life in buggy retreat centers, and Burning Man looks too hot and dusty for my taste. At MEA, I could sleep each night snuggled in high-thread-count sheets after making my own talking stick earlier and learning the spiritual practice of smudging with the healing power of palo santo. I could, though I graciously declined, say yes to invitations to cacao suppers and surf lessons.

One of my favorite features of the MEA campus was its library, generously donated by MEA's entrepreneurial founder, Chip Conley. One afternoon when I was looking for an excuse *not* to work on this book, I took it upon myself to organize the school's vast dusty collection of books and was edified by the familiar titles that sit on my own shelves in my own coaching studio back in California:

Jon Kabat-Zinn. *Check.*
Julia Cameron. *Check.*
Martin Seligman. *Check.*
Pema Chodron. *Check.*
Viktor Frankl. *Check.*
William Bridges. *Check.*
Daniel Pink. *Check.*
Jay Shetty. *Check.*
Ryan Holiday. *Check.*
Kristin Neff. *Check.*
Joseph Campbell. *Check.*
Parker Palmer. *Check.*
Jack Kornfield. *Check.*

MEA was to me the ultimate campus of tone setter wisdom. The nirvana. The place that none of us, even the most awesome of tone setters, fully realize in our lives. How often do we have the opportunity to engage with strangers in such a deep way, free of pesky agendas and power plays? During my two weeks in Baja with my loosely knit cohort, there were no photos shared of anyone's fabulous kitchen renovations, no rants about terrible bosses or heinous post-pandemic commutes. There was no griping about dysfunctional university administrations or the numbers of staff who quit, emboldened by the Great Resignation. There was no exaggerating one's privilege, and it was clear I was hanging with some incredibly well-heeled people. One held the title of countess! Instead, it was a time of splashing in the waves at nearby Cerritos Beach and of learning the precise art and strategy of stacking rocks. We watched brilliant red sunsets after dinner, and we stumbled out of our beds early in the morning as the sun illuminated the waves. We were liberated from what came before and what was to come. We were here on a splendid campus, right now.

As MEA completes construction on its second campus in Santa Fe, New Mexico, it plays a unique role in a growing roster of learning centers dedicated to the study of wisdom and designed for people nearing or past the point of retirement—people looking to make sense of their careers and establish a fulfilling path forward for the next chapter of their lives. Unlike MEA, most of these programs are being developed on existing college and university campuses, most famously at Stanford's Distinguished Careers Institute and Harvard's Advanced Leadership Institute. Other wisdom programs have joined the mix, including Notre Dame's Inspired Leadership Initiative, University of Minnesota's Advanced Career Initiative, UT-Austin's Tower Fellows, and University of Oxford's Next Horizons. Some schools are even leveraging the campus for cross-generational experimentation. Arizona State University's Lifelong University Engagement initiative accommodates over 450 elders who have moved into a campus community called Mirabella, an innovation to watch as our country's aging population is looking for more life-affirming alternatives to over-fifty-five gated country club communities.

A network has emerged to provide thought leadership to this growing higher education sub-industry. Called the Nexel Collaborative, this not-for-profit network of academics has created a base camp for college-based midlife transition programs designed to help learners renew their purpose, build new social networks, incorporate wellness practices, and foster intergenerational and community engagement.

PILLARS OF REPUTATIONAL WISDOM

James Clear writes that "reputation is the echo of your actions." Whereas the character wisdom traits described in the last chapter offer tone setter ways of being, reputational wisdom puts us in action. This is about ways of doing.

Pillar of Elasticity

The reputational pillar of elasticity exists when we say, "Sure, why not?" Like the time your student assistant begged you to be part of a flash mob at lunch in the dining hall, or the committee you graciously agreed to chair at the request of your vice president, or the journal article you coauthored that stretched you to the outer limits of your intellectual capacity. The truth is, even our most luminous tone setters willingly admit that they are comfort-seeking humans. But for these tone setters, there is a healthy tension between the cozy feeling of predictability and the dull lull of stagnation. Even with all the recent transformation in higher education, there are still plenty of areas operating in a time warp, and it can become all too easy to coast. Tone setters may cherish tradition, but they want to continue to grow, and they are all in for new challenges. Tone setters expand their reputational wisdom by stretching themselves, exercising their elasticity by saying yes to invitations for growth. Here are some examples:

- An innovative colleague of mine at Wake Forest University found himself on the TEDx stage, delivering a talk on higher education disruption that went viral, sending ripples of creative energy through the industry and turning him into a national thought leader.
- A longtime friend with an interest in emerging communications moved up through the administrative ranks at North Carolina State University and developed a podcast called *Wolfpack Career Chats*. She has hosted and produced over 300 episodes, and *Wolfpack* has been downloaded over 50,000 times.

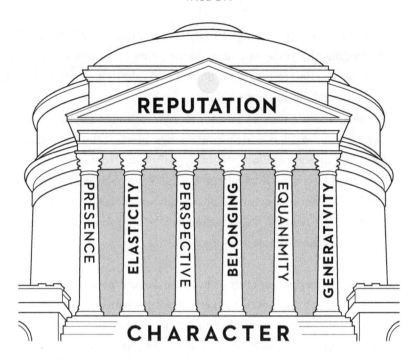

- A multifaceted client from Sonoma State University gave up the Northern California wine country for LA, taking on an expansive new administrative role while caring for three children under the age of six.
- A high-performing direct report of mine resigned from my staff at UC San Diego and moved to the United Arab Emirates to start up a new student services office at a brand-new campus being built by New York University in Abu Dhabi.
- A board colleague decided upon retirement from Georgia State University that she had more to contribute professionally. She applied for and was admitted into the prestigious Next Horizons program at Oxford. Her research provided the foundation for a consulting practice she founded upon her return to the United States.
- A mentor at UC Berkeley managed a growing, nationally recognized student center while volunteering with a national team of volunteers to launch a game-changing technology for how students learn about and apply for postgraduate jobs.

- A client from Binghamton University expanded her influence by overseeing the build-out of a donor-named campus center and then proceeding to take on a portfolio of additional organizations, budgets, and administrative duties.
- A colleague with a keen knack for reorganization to improve impact deepened his skill as a high-level change agent at the University of Florida, Carnegie Mellon, Stanford, and Johns Hopkins.
- A client at UNLV cut her teeth on the Las Vegas campus before growing her impact at University of Arizona and UC Merced. Decades after she left Nevada, she returned to UNLV in a senior leadership position as the ultimate wisdom worker.

You and I can probably think of countless examples of wise, elastic tone setters on our campuses. In every case, tone setters seize moments of opportunity, moving beyond their comfort zones to try new things. They give themselves permission to lean into risk in order to achieve new aspirations that align with their values. Elasticity isn't just about pursuing promotions. It is more a growth mindset that calls us to add value in new ways, to explore the reaches of our capacity, and to stay fresh and in motion.

Pillar of Belonging

I have a beautiful Zen chime that I carry with me when I facilitate campus retreats. The chime was a gift from Deb Chereck, a charismatic tone setter from the University of Oregon and past president of my association. Deb gave me the chime when I became president of the same association, urging me to use it at board meetings to call fellow board members back from breaks. I used the chime for that very purpose, and since then it has traveled with me throughout the world. Teams that I facilitate appreciate the soothing sound of the mindful gong. For me, the sound takes me back to a time when, as an incoming volunteer leader, I was anxious, saboteurs of limitation all around. The chime, and the mentor who gave it to me, provided me with a cherished sense of belonging.

Tone setters like Deb make people feel good, like they are at home. They are known for engaging people from many different backgrounds. Wise tone setters become known for deepening their relationships throughout their campus communities. They take the time to connect with people in divisions that are not their own. They know the names of colleagues' spouses and kids. They are aware of people's pending surgeries. They send emails or written cards to note others' accomplishments. My boss once sent me a handwritten note through campus mail when I was elected to a higher education board. I still have it! She was also known to throw an annual summer party at her home, giving her colleagues and direct reports an opportunity to meet her partner and her cats, and to experience her as much more than a senior campus administrator. Such leaders make higher education administration about so much more than a mere job for pay. Their strategy does not overtake their humanity. They remind us that in the end, college and university administration is a people business.

Pillar of Generativity

When psychoanalyst Erik Erikson coined the term "generativity" in 1950, he was describing a way to transcend our personal interests to provide care and concern for younger and older generations. Today, we think of generative tone setters on our campuses as wisdom workers who create and maintain systems, programs, and policies that not only meet the current needs of their institutions but also anticipate and address future challenges and opportunities. They are establishing their legacy by drawing from their souls, not their egos. And they are applying many of the principles and mindsets laid out in this book.

Rachel Naomi Remen, MD, author of the *New York Times* bestseller *Kitchen Table Wisdom,* writes, "Helping, fixing, and serving are three different ways of seeing life. When you help, you see life as weak. When you fix, you see it as broken. When you serve, you see life as whole." Tone setters, without question, are drawn to serve. It's not merely giving back for the sake of fame or recognition. It is about taking actions that create pathways for others to crystallize their wisdom. It is about getting out of the way.

How do our campus tone setters demonstrate generativity?

- They exercise visionary leadership. They inspire others with an optimistic and achievable view of the future. By setting ambitious goals and articulating a compelling vision, tone setters rally support for innovative initiatives.
- They promote collaboration by encouraging interdisciplinary effort among campus stakeholders as well as partnerships with external organizations and industry stakeholders.
- They empower those around them. Generative tone setters clear the way for those in their sphere to take initiative and pursue innovative ideas. They create opportunities for professional development, provide support for experimentation, and recognize and reward creative contributions.
- They embrace technology which plays a crucial role in driving innovation in higher education. Generative tone setters champion emerging technologies and leverage them to enhance teaching and learning, streamline administrative processes, and improve student services.
- They adapt to change. Recognizing the importance of adaptability in a rapidly changing environment, they are proactive in identifying and responding to emerging trends, disruptions, and opportunities. By being agile and responsive, tone setters thrive in the face of uncertainty.
- They fully engage stakeholders. There are so many to keep in mind: students, alumni, parents, employers, and others. By soliciting feedback, fostering dialogue, and building partnerships, administrators can ensure that their initiatives are aligned with the needs and priorities of the broader community.

Our college campuses have the distinction of benefiting from the creativity energy of five generations—from the silent (1928–1945) to baby boomers (1946–1964) to Generation X (1965–1980) to millennial (1981–1996) and Generation Z (1997–2010). And across these generations, there are tone setters who share their wisdom rather than hold onto it. Tone setters don't become cranks or old codgers. There is no "back in my day" mentality. Tone setters see an expanding world before them (growth mindset). They are not contained by their campuses. Their schools become launch pads for new ideas, innovations. They are wisdom seekers, not simply wisdom keepers.

SECURING OUR ROOFLINE

Whereas tone setter pillars of character wisdom—presence, perspective, and equanimity—provide the strong foundation for our wisdom principles, the reputational pillars of elasticity, belonging, and generativity connect with the sky. They can be seen from afar. They take our crystalized wisdom and actualize it for all to experience.

CONCLUSION

I am the me I choose to be.

—SIDNEY POITIER

"To WRITE A great book, you must first become the book." How true this quotation from Naval Ravikant is, especially as I complete this manuscript with stacks of handwritten letters, sorted by decade on the credenza behind me. The letters were from my father the college professor, Abba Cep as his students and colleagues called him. They were written to his only brother, my Uncle Florian, between the 1940s and the 1990s and were saved and sent to me by my cousin following my uncle's passing at 102, years after my father passed at the age of 84. I spent an unusually late night reading through dozens of letters, my dad's sweeping cursive covering the pages with details of our family and of his career.

Dad was hired in 1949 at a fledgling college in Center City, Philadelphia, which had no accreditation at the time, offered only associate's degrees, and was housed in a former YMCA. As I read through his letters to his brother, I appreciated anew his forty-year career at that college, all the milestones the institution achieved, and all the contributions he made to the college and its students. In one of his letters, my dad inserted a folded student newspaper from April 1967. I learned from one of its articles that it was through the financial generosity of the junior class and the college's alumni association that my Abba Cep, along with our mother, my three older brothers, and me at age five, were able to spend an entire year in Jerusalem while my father pursued his study sabbatical. The year was monumental for all of us, even me in the first grade at an Anglican

Church School. For dad, it led to deeper purpose as he gained expertise in the Middle East, expanding his understanding of its glorious history and bloody conflicts. For the remainder of his higher education career, he developed and led over thirty tours, taking hundreds of students, colleagues, and community members to Israel. For Abba Cep, these tours marked the pinnacle of his career. For him, his life's work emanated from the alchemy in a growing academy, an academy that discovered him and allowed him to make a living and build a life.

For anyone reading this today who is right in the middle—in the middle of your hierarchy, your career, your life—I know this can be an unnerving phase to navigate. Higher education careers aren't as gentle as they once were in my father's era. That's an understatement. Pensions and retirement schemes aren't the goldmines they once were. Challenging discussions around diversity, artificial intelligence, and freedom of speech are weathering our ivy-covered walls. Fundraising has become a relentless priority for our presidents and massive development staffs. Campus administrative jobs feel less stable as schools compete with one another for dwindling numbers of college-age students. Administrative change is a constant reality.

Yet, there is plenty of promise. The pandemic has liberated us from exclusively bricks-and-mortar learning, creating opportunity for countless students, faculty, and administrative staff to engage with higher education in a more customized and convenient manner. Our industry is transforming from dated paradigms of learning and service delivery to new approaches that leverage emerging technology and an agile breed of administrative leaders, tone setters who ride the waves of change while taking in the sheer beauty as they surf to the shore.

How about you? I suggest that college administration is a good fit for you if you have the capacity to be a tone setter in these areas:

1. You are adept at making order from chaos.
2. You are creative at generating financial, human, and physical resources to broaden impact.

3. You see challenges and conflict as opportunities to produce incremental change and bring people together in service of a higher mission.

4. You lean into new technologies and surround yourself with people who can help you leverage them.

5. You cut through process bumps and red tape with precision, breaking down barriers and reducing sludge.

6. You bolster relationships and partner with people, on campus and off, who fuel you with energy, strategy, and optimism.

7. You hold it all with a gentle grasp and keep your ego in check.

8. You take each success and bump in the road as gifts to grow your wisdom.

As I coach my treasured college and university clients, I am reminded of the awesome privilege I have to drop into their lives and onto their campuses. I still get to visit them on their splendid campuses, which I cherish, and I get to Zoom with them from my small coaching studio in Palm Springs, California. This is the work of quiet and confidential conversations, each one unique, focused, and memorable. Some of my clients are anxious. Many are uncertain. Others are determined. I learn from each and every one of them, and through them I am reminded each day of the high hopes and good intentions that bring people to this work. My job is to help them remember those hopes and intentions and live them boldly and fully, to become those tone setters who put out a sense of effortlessness, making it look so much easier than it really is.

Tone setters get the importance of individual moments in their campus lives. They may have an orchestrated strategy, but that does not numb them to how darn interesting the day-to-day actually is. Most likely, we only get to play this particular campus role just once. And we owe it to our organization and to ourselves to experience it completely: the ups, the downs, and the countless contributions made and lessons learned. Our race for rapid impact is a whole lot sweeter when we experience it in real time, all of it.

The places and people that inspired this book share a nuance, a subtlety that makes them extraordinary. They may not be influencers, well-known by the masses. But their presence makes an individual impact on all who experience their tone. We can't place that felt impact in a review on Yelp, Tripadvisor, LinkedIn, or a Qualtrics Net Promoter Scorecard. It lives in the experiences absorbed and decisions made by those of us who by happenstance found ourselves face-to-face with them.

Early in my career, I didn't realize I would get professionally side-tracked, meander into a university's student services office and apply for a job there. It didn't occur to me that I could build a fascinating career on a college campus or fall in love with its wonderful peculiarities. I didn't know what a university administrator was, and I never dreamed that title would open up the world for me, enable me to realize meaningful impact, and experience a deep professional and personal fulfillment.

In a recent interview on NPR's *Fresh Air* program, former Harvard University president Drew Gilpin Faust reflected on the role of colleges and universities. She remarked, "Education is about making people different, making them greater versions of themselves, providing them with capacity." For those of us who spend our lives adding value on college and university campuses as members of the administrative staff, we are on both the sending and receiving end of that sentiment. And if we truly sink into our campus lives, over time we become inspired, fulfilled, and wise tone setters in the academy.

EPILOGUE

NOT LONG AGO, Skip and I were in Pennsylvania for a wedding, and we had some time to kill before suiting up for the blessed event. So we did what we often do when on the road. At my urging, we stepped out of our hotel and set our navigation on the nearest college campus to complete the inevitable scavenger hunt for a visitor parking spot and sniff our way into a student café. Our objective was to score free Wi-Fi and to hot desk for a few hours. It had been over a decade since I took the stage in Orlando representing my higher education association and over thirty years since I gazed down at the University of Virginia from Thomas Jefferson's mountaintop at Monticello, so uncertain about any future that might exist for me as a higher education administrator. It turned out, there was a future, well beyond my imagination. Skip and I have been tag-teaming from campus to campus ever since, renewing our commitment to higher education again and again, one campus engagement at a time.

A table by the window of the Blue Line Café at Lancaster's Franklin & Marshall College was the perfect perch to open up our MacBooks, take in the colorful fall foliage, and watch the parade as students, faculty, and staff poured in for their morning jolts. Members of the F&M community are called Diplomats, we learned as we watched students with their Uggs, flannel lounge pants, and messy top knots. How was it that after all these years it all felt the same, down to the too-loud 70s headbanger music blasting through the café's sound system? The only difference between then and now was in the students' eyes, focused not on each other or even the work-study student barista taking their orders but instead peeled intently on screens in their hands.

I had no interest in checking my texts, choosing to glance instead at the cluttered café bulletin board while I waited for our lattes and breakfast sandwiches. The corkboard was lined with orange, gold, and red leaves cut out from construction paper and painstakingly stapled to create an autumnal border around an otherwise chaotic collage of thumbtacked flyers. One described the semester's Thursday common hours where diverse speakers were lined up to present on topics like *Lyrical Leadership*, *Who's Black and Why*, and *Inclusion Improves Innovation*. There was also an announcement for a special alumni talk on how students can *Fight the Opioid Crisis with Prevention*. Another promoted registration for F&M's True Blue Network Mentorship Program (take a picture of the QR code for additional information and requirements). A colorful *Do Good With Chipotle* poster encouraged the senior class to participate in their annual fundraiser.

On this beautiful fall day at F&M in the heart of Pennsylvania's Amish country, I was reminded that however much our campuses and the generations they educate and employ have changed, there are still the campus bulletin boards broadcasting the events, services, and agendas of so many who make these magical communities hum. And there are still gifted administrative tone setters—like my father, like me, and like you—ensuring that the magic of the academy happens with each incoming class of students.

ACKNOWLEDGEMENTS

I N JANUARY, 2022, I rented a one-room Airbnb over a garage along a scruffy alley in Long Beach, California, less than a mile from the campus of Cal State Long Beach. This would be my home base for the next three days. I had an idea for a book, and I needed an unfamiliar environment, a new campus to explore, and freedom from routine distractions to flesh it out and build an initial outline. *Tone Setters in the Academy* was born, and in the nearly three years since, the book and its author have benefited by many who propelled me forward to complete it. Each of them has their own stories about their higher education experience and those whose tone offered inspiration.

Early on, Chas Hoppe (BA and MA Western Washington University), helped me find my voice as an author and frame the book as a teaching memoir. Freelance editor Veronica Jauregui (BA University of Arizona) spent a summer with me meticulously reviewing the full draft while coaching me to strengthen my arguments. Author and founder of the Rising Authors community, Hussein Al-Baity (BA Portland State University), provided a free, vibrant community for authors to share best practices and power through the ups and downs of nonfiction writing. Hal Clifford of Avocet Books (BA Dartmouth College) rescued my manuscript after the implosion of my first publisher. Hal's editorial, production, and design teams elevated the quality and presentation of the book. In particular, Avocet editor Brian Hurley (BA UC San Diego, MA Emerson College), patiently led me through several drafts of the book. He kept me on schedule while oh so gently nudging me to "kill my darlings." The book is shorter, tighter, and more readable thanks to Brian. Just when I thought my manuscript was squeaky clean, along comes proofreader and copy editor Michael Totten (BA University of Oregon). His painstaking edits kept me in Word track changes for days, and I thank him.

Writing is a quirky endeavor, and creative hits happen when they happen—while taking a walk, riding my bike, stretching on a yoga mat, or boarding a flight. It takes a special companion to ensure that I had the space and time to put the words on the page. And so, to my beloved of more than three decades, Skip Horne (BSFS Georgetown University, MBA University of Virginia Darden School of Business), I thank you for your steady support and belief in me. We have passed through many campuses together, with more to come. I love you.

For all those I have named in this book, and for the countless other friends I have coached, served, and worked alongside, it is you whose tone inspires this book, and it is my hope that you see yourselves in its pages.

Author's Note

Tone Setters in the Academy is a collection of insights drawn from rich, lived experiences and the wisdom of many voices that have shaped my perspective on higher education. I have carefully credited ideas, theories, and sources to their original creators. The wisdom woven throughout this work reflects the profound contributions of numerous authors, thought leaders, and visionaries. The narratives recounted, the campuses explored, and the individuals depicted are authentic, though I have taken care to protect the identities of both past and present clients.

INDEX

inspiration 33, 38, 87, 95

intelligence 155

intentionality 162

internal competitors 113

intuition 103, 147, 150

J

Jacobsen, Mary 130

Jefferson, Thomas 29, 33, 89

The Jesuit Guide to (Almost) Everything (Martin) 143

Johnson, Amy 162

Johnson, Lyndon 22

Joslin, Mitch 64, 65

Joy at Work (Kondo & Sonenshein) 96

K

Kabat-Zinn, Jon 96

Keltner, Dacher 91

Kennedy, John F. 22

key performance indicators (KPIs) 57

kintsugi 103

Kitchen Table Wisdom (Remen) 175

Knierim, Karen 34

Kondo, Marie 96

Kornfield, Jack 170

Kubler-Ross, Elisabeth 133

L

lagniappe 83

The Lean Startup (Ries) 120

Leider, Richard 45, 70

Lesser, Marc 70

liminality 140

S

Y

Z

ANDREW TRACY CEPERLEY has focused his thirty-five-year career on the transformative impact that a college education affords students and the campus and industry professionals who teach, advise, and mentor them. Andy has an extensive record of contribution in leader development, organizational realignment, team engagement, and program innovation by delivering a variety of integrated coaching, assessment, and strategic positioning services to colleges and universities and the individuals and teams that serve them.

Andy has served as Assistant Vice Chancellor at the University of California San Diego; Associate Provost at Loyola Marymount University; Associate Dean and Director at Santa Clara University; and several leadership roles at the University of Texas at Austin, University of Virginia, and Claremont McKenna College. Andy earned an administrative Fulbright to study higher education transformation in Germany and Poland in 2005. In 2013-14 he served on-site at the University of Melbourne in Australia, leading a campus-wide initiative to reimagine the institution's decentralized careers operations for students. And from 2014-2017, Andy served as expert consultant with the University of Iloilo, Philippines in the establishment of their inaugural Career Center.

Andy is a past president of the National Association of Colleges and Employers (NACE), and he was inducted into the highly selective NACE Academy of Fellows in 2016, in recognition of his impact on the profession.

He is an active Professional Certified Coach, a speaker, facilitator, author, and member of several associations, networks, and coaching organizations—including the International Coaching Federation, the PQ Positive Intelligence Community, and the Co-Active Training Institute where he earned his credential as a Certified Professional Co-Active Coach.

To learn more, visit *andrewtceperley.com.*